Exiles and Orphans

A Perry Family History

Kerri-Ann Price

2023

Foreword

Dear Reader,

I would like to share with you a story of an ordinary Australian family. This family history started in the United Kingdom and ended in the Central Victorian Goldfields.

Australia was inhabited before the white colonists decided that it was a great place for a penal settlement, however, this is the story of a couple who were sent here, because they were considered to be good stock to help build the new world.

This is the story of Edmund Perry and Ellen Gormley. Both were young adults when they were transported. They met, married and raised a large family. They may not have been famous, but, that is precisely the point of telling their story. These are the types of people that helped build Australia. They are our ancestors who shaped who we are today.

I wonder if their traumatic young lives had any generational effects? Studies have been carried out that suggests that this could be the case. We somehow carry the traumas of our ancestors in our DNA. This idea may help explain why people are they way they are. Why they vote a certain way. Why they react to different societal events the way they do. Why they are compliant or not. Why they believe what they believe.

Edmund and Ellen were my 4 x Great Grandparents on my fathers side.

All the information in this book comes from public sources. I'm sure there is way more to discover about The Perry's and their descendants, however this gives you a good sense of the family. I have no doubt that there are more people to be included, however, their information wasn't available to me. Perhaps you, could use my book as a start to further investigation.

I have tried to be very accurate and apologise in advance if you find an error.

I truly hope you enjoy reading this story and I hope I have imparted to you not just the facts but the atmosphere around the characters, to give us a sense of their lives.

Kind regards

Kerri-Ann Price

Contents

Edmund Perry

Edmund Perry was born in 1825 in the area of Nunton and Bodenham, Wiltshire, England. Edmund was the eldest son of George (1801-1847) and Elizabeth (nee Sparks) (1801-1878)and was named after his grandfather Edmund Perry (1765-1801).

Here is a photo of Bodenham taken in the 1800's

Below is a picture of George and Elizabeth's marriage certificate. It looks like George could write, however, Elizabeth made a mark rather than signing her name, so she mustn't have been able to read or write.

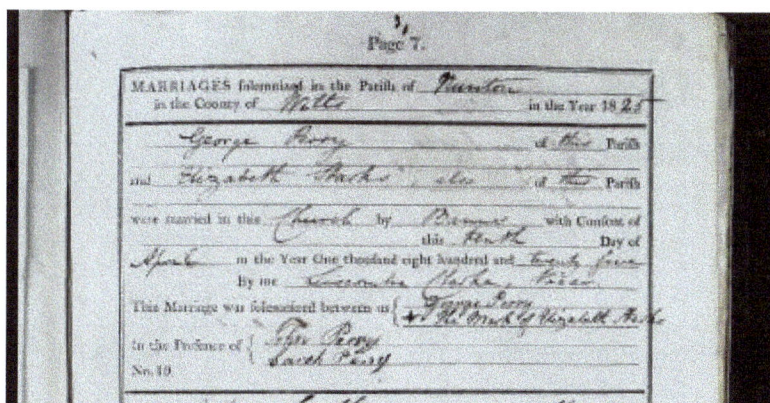

George worked as a Gardener and he won many prizes for his vegetables in 1830's according to articles in the newspapers.

Edmund had 8 siblings: Ann (1828-1905), Sarah (1830-1904), Mary (1832-bef1837), George (1833-1889), Maria (1835-1872), Mary (1837-1918), Elizabeth (1840-aft 1881) and Martha (1842-?).

Edmund was baptised 22nd May, 1825. Here is a picture of the registration.

In 1841, when Edmund was 16, he was working as a labourer. Here is a picture of the census, which shows the family. They were living in Bodenham Nunton and George is working as a Gardener.

In 1844 at the age of 19, Edmund along with John Gore of Bodenham and Nunton were charged with stealing 10 silver spoons, a coin (guinea) and other items, that belonged to Elizabeth Dowling. Edmund was sentenced to 7 years transportation. He is the bottom of page. I'm sorry if it's hard to read.

The following was found in the Salisbury and Winchester Journal 22 June, 1844.

(Hants).

*Committed to Fisherton Gaol :—*Edmund Perry and John Gore, of Bodenham and Nunton, charged with having feloniously stolen ten silver spoons, one gold coin called a guinea, and other articles, the property of Elizabeth Dowling. Stephen Cott, of Eling, charged with stealing a quantity of bark, the property of George Edw. Eyre, Esq. Chas. Williams, of Mere, charged with stealing a fowl, the property of Wm. Wickham. Chas. Conner, of Salisbury, for want of sureties to keep the peace, &c. Edmund Elderton, of Salisbury, for a month, for assaulting Elizabeth Barkett. Joseph Wells, of Shaftesbury, a

And this follow up article was found in the Bristol Mercury 13 July 1844

of September to the 10th of February, inclusive.

WILTS COUNTY SESSIONS.—The following prisoners were sentenced to ten years' transportion :—Henry Lawrence, for stealing a sheep at Mere ; Henry Scull, stealing above 5*l.*, belonging to a benefit society at Tinhead.—Seven years : Wm. Harding, stealing 75*l.* in notes and 11 sovereigns, &c. at Wilton ; Edmund Perry, stealing 10 silver spoons, a guinea, &c. at Bodenham and Nunton. The other prisoners were sentenced to various terms of imprisonment.

The inhabitants of Weston-super-Mare, Banwell,

Edmund received 7 years transportation sentence and was sent to a Pentonville prison for the first couple of years of the sentence. Edmund was 19 years old at the time. I know times were different then but I can't help thinking that 7 years is a very harsh sentence for stealing a few spoons.

10

Edmund was a Pentonvillian!

Here is more information about the Pentonville system and explains what Edmund endured.

Pentonville Model Prison was established with the aim of reforming convicts through religious exhortation, rigorous discipline and the imposition of separate confinement in its most extreme form.

Male convicts aged ideally between 18 and 25 and "with some promise" were to serve a probationary period of 18 months before dispatch to the Australian penal colonies. Their behaviour at Pentonville determined their place in the colonies with the best receiving tickets of leave. However, in 1849 the special status of Pentonville in the convict system was removed and it became a place for all male convicts to serve their probationary term (now reduced to 9 months), after which they would be transported abroad or sent to a public works prison. This function continued more or less until the decision to remove it from the convict prison system in 1885 and hand it over to the local prison authorities.

On arrival in Pentonville, prisoners were made to strip naked and their clothes and possessions were confiscated. They were then placed into a bath of waist-high water and carbolic acid and their heads were shaved and prisoners were not allowed to regrow hair until three months before the end of their sentence.

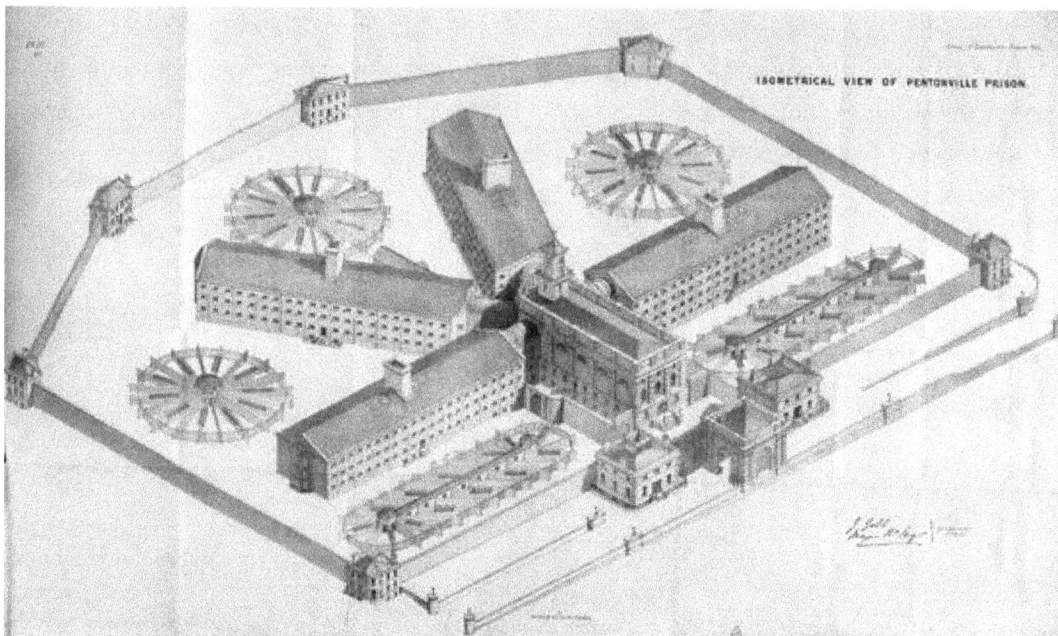

ISOMETRICAL VIEW OF PENTONVILLE PRISON.

Each prisoner would have his own cell measuring 13 feet (4 m) long, 7 feet (2 m) wide and 9 feet (3 m) high with little windows on the outside walls and an opening linking it to narrow landings in the galleries. Cells contained a table, a chair, a cobbler's bench, a hammock, a broom, a bucket and a corner shelf which held a pewter mug and dish, a bar of soap, a towel and a Bible.

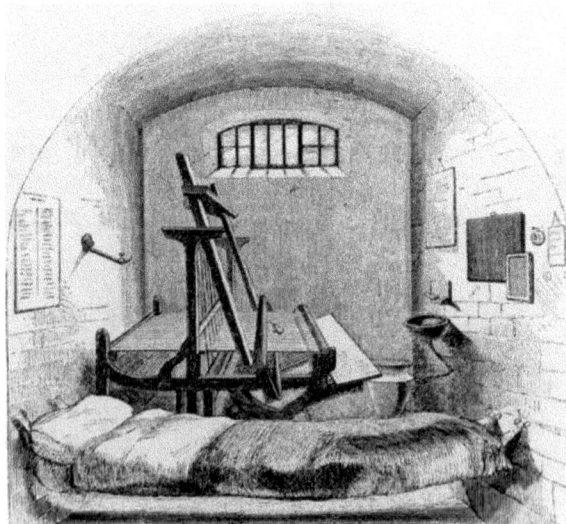

Diet consisted mainly of bread and water gruel. Prisoners received 10oz of bread at breakfast, 5 oz for lunch and a further 5oz for supper. Potatoes were often rotten and barely edible.

Prisoners were given compulsory doses of Potassium Bromide to subdue sexual urges which sometimes impacted on their mental health.

Prisoners were allowed one fifteen-minute observed visit every six months and one letter every six months which was censored by the warden and staff.

The convicts at Pentonville Prison were made to wear dark grey outfits with "P.P" embroidered in red into the collar.

CONVICTS.
(From Photographs by Herbert Watkins, 179, Regent Street.)
MALE CONVICT AT PENTONVILLE PRISON. | FEMALE CONVICT AT MILLBANK PRISON.

As a visitor wrote, "they were admirably ventilated with a water closet" (toilet), though these were replaced by communal, vile-smelling recesses because they were constantly blocked, and the pipes were sometimes used by prisoners to communicate.

The regime at Pentonville was predictably very rigid. From first light at 5.45am to lights out at 8pm, every aspect of the day was under scrutiny whether at work, during exercise or in the prison chapel.

Prisoners were isolated and worked, ate, and slept in their cells, spending almost twenty-three hours of each day there.

When not in their cells, prisoners were forced to wear caps with a mask and beak that covered their faces and were assigned numbers to replace their names in order to preserve anonymity.

When gathered for exercise in the prison yard, they had to hold onto long ropes knotted at 4.6-metre (15 ft) intervals so that they were unable to communicate.

Daily attendance for chapel services was mandatory, and each convict was confined to a separate booth, or "coffin" as the prisoners referred to them. Their heads were visible to the warder or clergyman but hidden from each other so that communication with fellow inmates was all but impossible. The only time prisoners were allowed to use their voices was when singing hymns.

THE CHAPEL, ON THE "SEPARATE SYSTEM," IN PENTONVILLE PRISON, DURING DIVINE SERVICE.

The Silent System existed alongside the Separate System. The main aim behind the Silent System was to protect prisoners from negative influences. A feature of the Silent System was to give prisoners boring and seemingly pointless tasks.

Oakum picking

Picking oakum was a way for able-bodied inmates to earn their board and lodging while keeping occupied for long periods. Prisoners serving hard labour would cut the rope into two-foot sections and then strike them with a heavy mallet to remove coats of hardened tar. It was passed to prisoners serving lesser sentences or who were deemed weaker, such as women and children, who had to uncoil, unravel, unpick, and shred the rope into fibres which would be re-used on sailing ships. The work was monotonous, unpleasant and caused sores on blackened fingers. There were some complaints that picking oakum was too comfortable as a punishment; the treadwheel was preferred.

Treadwheel

The treadwheel, also known as treadmill or "everlasting staircase" was first introduced in 1818 as a means of usefully employing prisoners. The device was a wide hollow cylinder, usually made of wooden steps built around a cylindrical iron frame and could occupy as many as 40 prisoners. As it rotated, each prisoner was forced to continue stepping along the series of planks. The power generated by the treadwheel was sometimes used to grind corn and pump water, although usually it served no purpose at all other than punishment.

The Crank

It was believed that having prisoners occupy the same space to work the treadwheel or pick oakum invited mingling and possible communication. Some prison officials noticed inmates hated a pointless task more than a meaningful one, which presented them with an alternative – the crank.

The crank was a device that stuck out of a small wooden box that was usually set on a table or pedestal in the cell. Inside the box was a drum or paddle that turned sand or rocks connected to an axle. The crank had a screw which warders could tighten or loosen depending on how much punishment they wanted to administer or often to seek redress or revenge on a prisoner. This earned warders the nickname "screws". Each crank had a counter which recorded the number of turns. An inmate had to reach a certain number of turns before they were allowed to do basics such as eat and sleep. Most were expected to make at least 10,000 rotations a day – 2,000 for breakfast, 3,000 each for lunch and dinner, and 2,000 more before bed. The crank was designed to exhaust prisoners mentally and physically.

"Keep your knees straight",

"Hold the shot out from your body",

"Lay that shot down quietly",

"No supper for you tonight".

– A prisoner recalling shot drill in a prison in the 1860s.

Shot-drill

Shot-drill was where heavy cannon-balls were passed from one to another down a long line of prisoners for no reason other than to occupy prisoners, exhaust them and to break their resolve.

A prisoner at each row end raises his hand and the passing of the heavy shot begins again. One hundred prisoners shuffle back and fore in silence. There were no voices except those of the warders.

Methods of punishment

As well as punishments involving hard labour, such as the treadwheel, crank and shot-drill, being meted out to prisoners, breaches of prison discipline would be dealt with harshly.

The most common offence was breaking the rules on silence, for which prisoners would be placed in leg irons for short periods, confined to their cell with reduced rations, denied exercise or have their remission cancelled.

Swearing at or assaulting warders would be dealt with harshly, often by whipping.

Between 1844 and 1849, the British government transported 1739 convict 'exiles' to the Port Phillip District of New South Wales. Unlike transportation that had occurred in other parts of Australia, the convicts sent to Port Phillip had served part of their sentence in London's Pentonville or Millbank prisons.

On arrival in Australia, they were given a conditional pardon, provided they didn't return to England within the term of their original sentence.

Pentonville prisoners spent the first 18 months of their sentence in silent solitary confinement, followed by a period of hard labour on public works. They were then transported to Australia.

The first Pentonville exiles were sent to Van Diemen's Land in 1844, but the prison system was overcrowded, and they were soon sent to work as squatters' labourers in Port Phillip. Some Port Phillip residents were outraged at convicts being dumped in their colony, but most squatters were in favour of importing more exiles as cheap labour.

In London, the Colonial Office listened to the demands of the squatters and over the next five years, 1727 exiles were sent to Melbourne, Geelong and Portland. There was also unofficial transportation of convicts from other colonies.

All of the 'Pentonvillians' were male, with an average age of 22 years - the youngest was 11. Nearly all were literate and many came from trade and manufacturing backgrounds.

Most of their offences were crimes against property, for which they received sentences of seven years or more. The Pentonvillians had a bad reputation, but much of it was undeserved.

Unlike earlier convicts who were required to work for the government or on hire from penal depots, the Exiles were free to work for pay, but could not leave the district to which they were assigned.

Throughout the 1840s, there was growing opposition to the Pentonvillians, as many people saw it as transportation by another name: In 1849, ships carrying exiles were not allowed to dock in Sydney and Melbourne, and were forced to land their convicts in Moreton Bay, Queensland. This effectively ended convict transportation to New South Wales, including the Port Phillip District.

What sort of men did the Pentovillians become after their treatment in the gaol system?

The following article was discovered in The Morning Chronicle dated 13 March, 1846. It describes the situation well.

I will transcribe it for you here:-

SEPARA TE CONFINEMENT.-ITS RESULTS. To THE EDITOR OF THE MORNING CHRONICLE.

Sir--As the good or evil of separate confinement is now much in question and yesterday debated in the Court of Aldermen, you will, perhaps, allow me to bring forward an important piece of evidence on this subject, which is to be found in the papers on Van Diemen's Land lately laid before Parliament. The results are far from satisfactory, for on embarking 300 or 400 convicts from Pentonville, the superintending surgeon describes those men as falling into strong convulsions on their first coming on board, and in which they continued for four days. Infinite care and kindness did, after that period, restore them, but nevertheless their seclusion, though not of more than eighteen months at the maximum, had so impaired their faculties, that, docile and obedient to the highest degree, they could not understand the plainest directions for settling them in their berths ! This, too, is the report of a person who favours the system, and is, in spite of these distressing facts, disposed to continue it.

"Strong convulsions and a partial imbecility among nearly 400 exiles, as the new term runs, weighs not with him, but will, perhaps, in public opinion be esteemed as injurious and dangerous, particularly if this kind of discipline is to be established in every county in England. I must remark that these exiles were chosen subjects: had been treated with infinite care by the chaplain and surgeon on the voyage; were almost petted; for many diversions were offered, and among them the editing of a newspaper.

Their treatment recalled that of Parry to his crews then in the Polar seas, with the omission possibly of acting plays. These extraordinary indulgences cannot, however, be blamed though so unusual for it became necessary to rouse the torbid and half-extinct faculties into healthy action;in short, to undo, by every stimulant, the baneful effects of separate imprisonment. Reformed they also were, but without energy, with impaired comprehension, teachable and tractable, but unfitted for the of settlers, which demands more than any other "the mens sana in compore sano." Meekness, humility, and contrition do not qualify men whose lot is that severe one of taming the wilderness, and making the desert smile with cultivation. The bush calls for the best energy of the hardiest emigrant, and will not endure the penitent in shady cloister long immured, nor the docile recluse. But I will rather follow the course of these men than break into comment. Their voyage of four months was long and pleasant. On their arrival, their fair characters secured them without difficulty, situations in the colony. But after five more months, the governor, Sir Eardley Wilmot, thus writes of them.: " They are obedient and willing, but greatly depressed, probably from their peculiar treatment at home, and are without energy." Nevertheless, he too is a convert to the system, in spite of his strong testimony against it.

Possibly the governor will see reason to change this opinion, when he shall have received some thousands of these exiles, whose morals will have been acquired at the expense of their understanding and energy. Your obedient servant, P.

On 26 June 1846 Edmund embarked "The Maitland" As the ship record states …. "These convicts were embarked from Millbank, Parkhurst and Pentonville prisons for the purpose of proceeding after their arrival of Hobart Town to Geelong in Port Phillip under conditional pardons." I wonder how Edmund fared aboard?

The Maitland

According to Lloyds Register, the Maitland was a Malabar teak, three deck, thee mast sailing passenger/cargo vessel of 755 tons, 126 feet (38.6m) in length, 34 feet (10.5m) beam and 23 feet waterline to keel. Recorded as a 'Blackwall Frigate', she was built at the J & R Kyd Blackwall Shipyard in Calcutta, India in 1810 and launched 4 November, 1811. Her crew varied but averaged 90 men.

The Maitland had a colourful sixty year sailing history. She voyaged for the East India Company between 1812-30 combined cargo, passengers and occasional 'Privateering' or officially sanctioned pirating, made her first migrant voyage in 1838 which resulted in highly critical Committee of Inquiry findings against the owners and officers. The vessel next transported British and Irish convicts from Britain to Tasmania/Van Diemen's Land between 1840-46. She once again switched business models as the transport of convicts began to become less acceptable and returned to the more lucrative market of transporting migrants from Britain to Australia for two voyages in 1849-1855. Due to her age and uneconomic size, the Maitland spent her final years shipping cargo on the Mediterranean trade until wrecked at a location unspecified in 1869.

The Maitland's final voyage as a convict transporter was one of twelve ships that transported convicts from Britain to the Australian colonies in 1846 and Edmund was on board.

The Maitland sailed from Portsmouth on the 22nd June 1846 carrying 299 men, none sentenced to life and the others with an average sentence of 9 years. Docking at Port Phillip on 27th October 1846, some researchers understand that 291 of the prisoners were disembarked and the Maitland then sailed on to Hobart with the remaining six prisoners. Other researchers believe that all of the prisoners were disembarked at Port Phillip. So Edmund had arrived in Australia.

There was an article in the Geelong Advertiser and Squatters Advocate on 11 November 1846. Here is what the article says:

The exile ship Maitland, which has been so long looked for by the settlers of this district has arrived at Melbourne. We have all along been led to beieve, that the exiles brought by her would be landed at Geelong; and even had no implied pledge to this effect existed, we might reasonably have looked to such an arrangement as the best which could have been made for the benefit of the men them-selves. We believe that the government is willing to forward them to Geelong, upon condition of the Immigration Society taking charge of them upon disembarkation on the wharf. No doubt the Society will be glad to do so rather than lose the men; but the conduct of the government in making such a stipulation is excessively paltry. Such of the exiles as may be willing to come on to Geelong (for we believe that, from the time of casting anchor they become free agents, and their future

movements voluntary) will be brought down by the steamers during the next day or two. The exiles ap-pear to be a somewhat heterogenous muster, as will appear from the following notice in an English paper, but the worst characters have of course been de-tained in Van Diemen's Land: The English ship Mait-land arrived at Portsmouth, for the purpose of receiving on board about 70 of the incorrigibles from Parkhurst; altogether, there are 190 convicts on board, for Van Diemen's Land, among them, it is said, is the notorious Captain Johnson, of the Tory, also about 100 convicts under 25 years of age. The juveniles will embark so soon as the order from the Secretary of State reaches the Governor of Parkhurst. The whole will be under the charge of ninety soldiers.

THE MAITLAND — This vessel has brought 299 men from the Pentonville Penitentiary and Parkhurst Prison. They are, we understand, excellent men, and any one requiring servants will be allowed to go on board and select them as soon as they have been inspected by the Superintendent or some one appointed by him.

Port Phillip Gazette and Settlers Journal

11 November 1846

Edmund was transported with a number of other convicts that had been through the Pentonville system, but aboard was another group, just as interesting in a historical sense. The other group were Parkhurst boys. These boys are worth a mention in Edmunds story.

Between 1842 and 1852 about 1500 boys between the ages of 12 and 18 were transported to Australia from the Parkhurst Juvenile Prison on the Isle Of Wight. The Parkhurst prison was run along very similar lines to the Pentonville system, therefore, would have affected the boys in many ways both positive and negative. The boys were taught trades such as bricklaying. Most of the Parkhurst boys were sent to Western Australia, however, there were about 70 of them aboard the Maitland that arrived in Port Phillip Bay.

The article pictured was published in The Melbourne Argus on 24 November, 1846. I found it interesting because it was an event that happened whilst Edmund was still aboard The Maitland. I have transcribed this article over the next couple of pages.

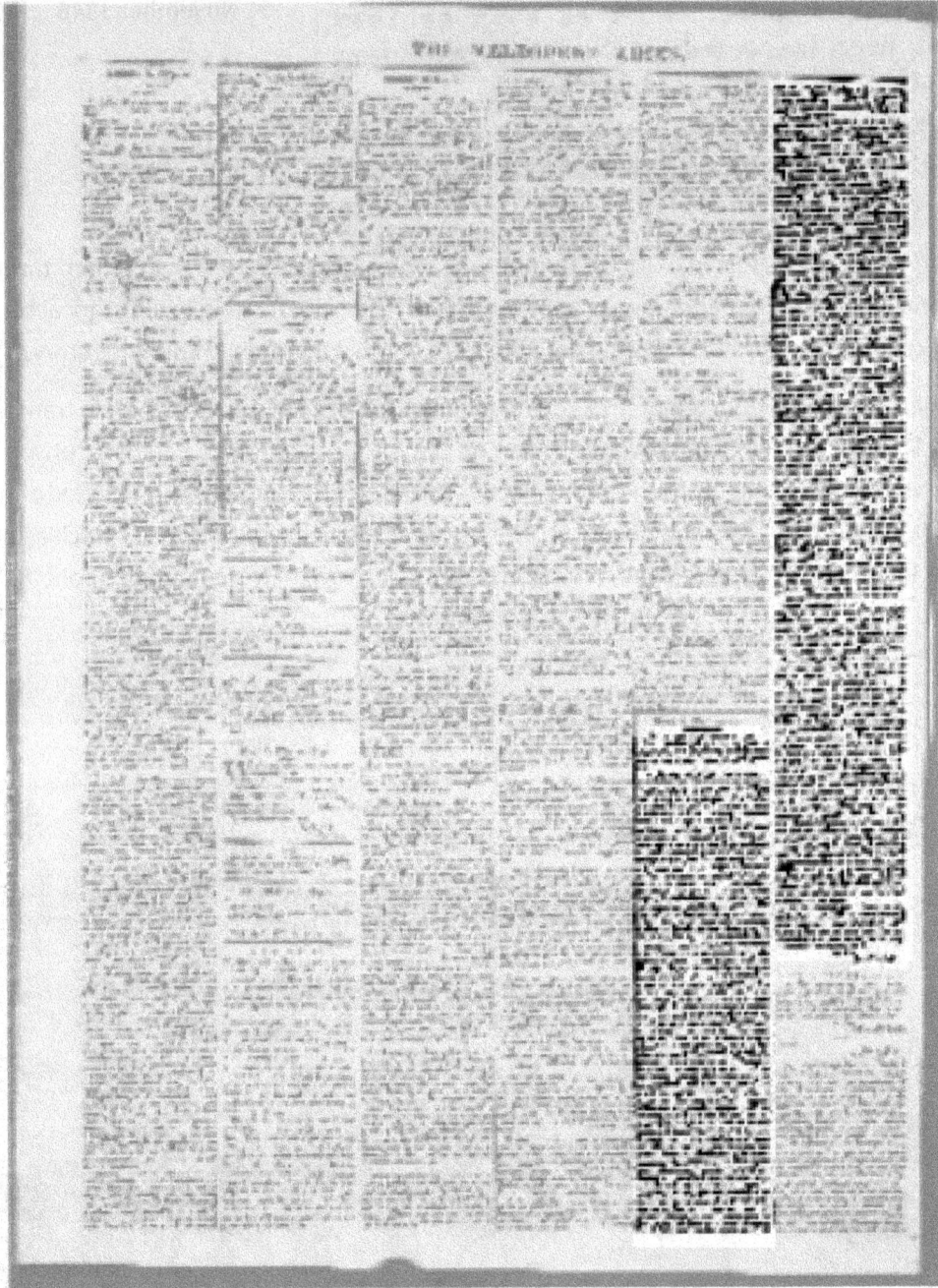

To the Editor of the Melbourne Argus.

Sir-I shall feel obliged if you will publish in your next number the following detailed account of the circumstances which induced me to appear as a plaintiff before the Police bench on Friday last.

On the afternoon of the 11th November, I proceeded on board the Maitland, (at anchor in Hobson's Bay,) in company with Mr. William Nicholson, and Mr. Robert Mouat ; at Liardet's Mr. Crossley joined us, we proceeded to embark, and before putting off, Mr. Webster, the snuff manufacturer, and Mr. Patterson, shoemaker, came up and shipped in the same boat.

Upon our arrival on board the vessel, I found the doctor, (recognizable by his gold band on cap) and stating that I wished to engage a few people asked him if there were any rough carpenters on board, he answered he believed there were ; I thereupon desired that they might be brought to me, the doctor took the trouble to fetch me a man, whom he represented as being a carpenter, but that he had also the trade of a miller, and that he might probably wish to employ himself that way in preference to a carpenter, (which trade he learned in Pentonville prison ; I then stated that it was not in my power to find him such employment, and asked him if he would engage with me as carpenter , he replied he would ; I then asked him the rate of wages he would go for, but he, I think, did not name any rate ; I then offered him £20 per annum, which he at once refused, no other men were brought to me

I subsequently made enquiry amongst the younger class on board (that is the Parkhurst boys,) and ultimately founded my choice upon a youth aged 17 years. In the commencement of our treaty I asked him the rate of wages he required, his answer was, £16 ; I told him I would not give it him, but if he thought proper to engage with me as a general servant, I would take him for one year at £15, and would give no more, which he refused. He subsequently came to me and after further conversation he agreed to accept my terms, and hired with me.

I thereupon took him to the person in the cabin engaged in writing agreements, and stated that I had hired the boy at £15 for one year as a general servant. The clerk wrote the document, which was first signed by the boy, and afterwards by myself ; the clerk then took it to the cabin table, where a number of persons were seated and brought it back with him delivering it to me. I did not then notice what other stage it had undergone.

This completed, I said to the boy, now if you have got any acquaintance on board that you would wish to go with you, if you can say he is a good boy, upon seeing him, and if I approve of him, and he is willing to engage with me upon the same terms, I will take him also ; the boy returned stating that he had not found any that wished to go ; the boy's answer was given in the presence of others of the boys, on hearing which out came a boy of the name of Simmonds I think, and said, he would hire with me on the same terms. I asked him what he could do, his answer was-nothing. I remarked he could not profess to do less; I then asked him how he was employed previous to becoming a prisoner , he stated as a bricklayer ; I asked could he build a decent rough wall, he said, yes, either in brick or stone. I then agreed to take him, and proceeded to the clerk as before, and the agreement was nearly ready for signature when the doctor came to the desk and enquired-what's that, what's that-and then addressing me enquired if I had engaged the boy; he then asked the rate of wages ; I answered I him £15, he replied he shall not go out of this ship for that, but if I chose to give him £16 he might go; I replied I would not give one farthing more; his reply was as before, he shall not go out of this ship, and he instructed the clerk to destroy the agreement.

I then asked the doctor if I was to understand that he was to arbitrate the rate of wage betwixt me and my servants ; he replied he shall not go for less than £16. I replied that I supposed in this instance it must be as he determined, but I begged to state to him that I had also engaged another boy at the same rate; to this he replied as before, and referring to the clerk's list, ordered him to score the name out.

I then stated to him that in this case I felt myself in a very different position ; that I held in my possession a document which gave me at least a legal hold of the boy, notwithstanding his refusal to let him go; he enquired of the clerk if such document had been completed, and the answer was in the affirmative.

The doctor for the time was quieter, and seemed to doubt his power and retired to the cabin table. I afterwards entered the cabin, with hat in hand, and begged to have another word with the doctor, whereupon he gave an order to put me out; to this I replied I begged his pardon, I did not come to give insult or to be ungentlemanly; I merely wished to state my sentiments regarding the agreement with the boy Simmonds, which were, that notwithstanding I had not obtained a written agreement for him, yet I considered him virtually my servant.

I then retired and ordered the boy Ryder into the boat, and to take his traps with him, which order he complied with. A short time after this Mr, Erskine came upon the deck from the cabin and asked me could he have a word with me ; I answered certainly, Sir ; we both made to the captain, when be stated to me, that as he understood I considered I held a legal claim to the boy Ryder, he wished to undeceive me, and stated that I was probably not aware that the boy was a prisoner of the Crown; I replied that I was not, and I "did not care whether he was or no, that the vessel had been thrown open for the public to come and engage servants, but I was not aware that any officials on board had the power to arbitrate the rate of wages, and that I would not give up my claim to the boy.

He then stated that the boy would be sent after and taken out of my boat; I there-upon enquired if he stated what was intended to be done, which his reply confirmed. I observed that if that was the course intended, it would save trouble to all parties that this boy should be ordered by the Doctor out of the boat and on deck.

Such order was given by the Doctor to the Master, who instructed the mate to put it into effect, but notwithstanding he saw it properly executed.

Upon the boy's coming again on board, he was brought to the Doctor, who asked him if he was willing to go with me? The boy replied in the negative evidently from fear. Here the affair rested.

I was standing near the gangway afterwards, when the Master spoke to me, stating that he was Captain, and if I had anything more to say he would have me put overboard. Oh! are you the Master, I said, for hitherto since coming on board, I had not been able to discriminate which was the Master, but now he was at liberty to put his threat into execution; I stood some time, and turning round to the Master said, I probably could leave the vessel when I chose? he replied yes.

In a few minutes I again addressed him—I suppose I can go now as it is my wish? he again answered yes, and I went over the gangway. I understand that on my disappearing the Master gave orders to the Mate to 'mark' me and take care that I did not come on board the vessel again whilst she remained in harbour.

I think it now necessary to state that at the time the boy Ryder was ordered out of the boat and on deck, that two other boys were ordered up, one engaged by Mr. R Mouat, at £12 per annum, and one by Mr. W. Nicholson at £15 subsequently these boys were allowed to return to the boats, but my servant, Ryder, was forcibly detained, and shipped along with others for Geelong by the steamer the following morning.

On the 12th inst. Mr. Erskine was passenger in our boat to the beach; on the voyage the subject was again mooted, and, as another obstacle to my right, he made the assertion that the clerk was also a prisoner; I replied it appeared to me that the concern had commenced in villains, and villains were carrying it through ; he replied, if enquired into the villainy would be found on the other side.

On the 13th, I saw Mr. Erskine in Collins street, leading his horse, and made my way to him, asked him if I could speak a word with him ; he answered yes. I then asked him if he did not recollect saying to me the day but one previous, on board the Maitland, that the boy Ryder was a prisoner of the Crown ? He replied yes. I then asked him if he had no knowledge that on the day previous to his making such assertion the prisoners on board had been proclaimed free by the Superintendent, and that each and all of them had their tickets of freedom dated that day, the 10th instant?

Mr. L. then stated that he wanted nothing further to say with me upon the subject, and bid me go away. I then told him the affair should not rest there; he answered you may go and be d-d. I still said that I would first go to the Superintendent, and then take my own course, he again answered me you may go and be d-d, offering threats as to what he would do with me.

.

I wished him to complain, and let me see what he intended doing, he at length said he would give me in charge to the police this I dared him to, and told him I would make it a dear affair for him; he then ordered me off the street ; I did not obey his mandate ; he then asked me if I considered myself a gentleman? I answered certainly, but not such an one as to tell another in the street to go and be d-d.

It may be worthy of remark, that on the 10th a boy was hired for £12, and taken away, and numbers came on shore by the steamer which I found alongside the vessel without any written agreement, but some of which were hired, not withstanding that their masters did not deign to consult any authority on board.

I am, &c.

L. ROSTRON

IMPORTANT.—On Friday last Mr. L. Rostron, through his solicitor Mr. Ross, brought before the police bench, consisting of the Mayor and Mr. Alderman Russell, a young Pentonvillain, or Parkhurst youth, named Edward Ryder, charged with non-fulfilment of agreement under the Masters and Servants Act. The circumstances of the case are fully detailed in Mr. Rostron's letter which appears in another column. Dr. Robinson, surgeon-superintendent of the *exiles* on their passage, set up a claim, in his own person, of guardianship over the importations by the *Maitland*, commencing, we presume, upon his taking charge on board, but when terminating did not appear. The bench, however, refused to recognise the worthy Doctor's assumption, which they did not find warranted in law, and directed the boy to return to Mr. Rostron's service, whereupon Mr. Ross came forward, and on behalf of his client, who, he said, had brought the matter forward solely for the public protection, signified his willingness to cancel the agreement, which was accordingly done.

And here is the outcome, after the matter had gone before the courts.

This article was found in the "Melbourne Argus" on

24 November, 1846

28

There was a notice in the Melbourne Argus on 27th October, 1846.

The *Maitland*, convict ship, with a number of Parkhurst boys on board, sailed from Portsmouth for Van Diemen's Land on the 29th June. The Parkhurst beauties are said to be for Port Phillip.

According to the convict records the following information is recorded on Edmund upon arrival in the colony.

20 years old
Could both read and write
Occupation was Carter
Taught Shoemaking in prison
Single
Convicted of a Felony
Sentence 7 years

I found the following article in the Port Phillip Gazette and Settlers Journal 11 November, 1846. It's interesting to read because it gives us an idea of how the Pentonville and Parkhurst exiles were thought of in Australia. I have transcribed the article for you to read:

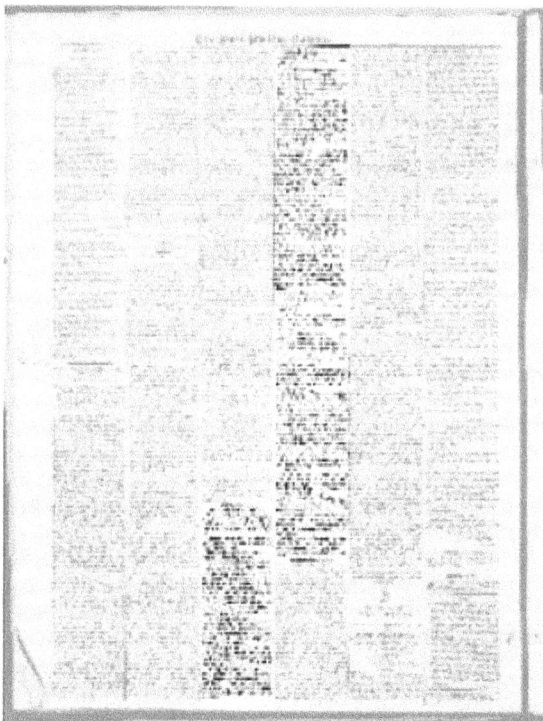

Legislative Committee.
Present : William Charles Wentworth, Esq., in the Chair; Dr. Bland, Henry Dangar, Esq., Richard Windeyer, Esq., John F. L. Foster, Esq., H. Macarthur, Esq. Alexander Sprot Esq., examined by the Chairman :
You are a squatter at Port Phillip? I am. How long have you been living in that district? About four years.
Can you state to what extent the freed and the conditionally pardoned convicts of Van Diemen's Land have come in upon you lately ; have you any idea of the numbers that have poured in since the system began ? Upwards of 1800 have, I think, come in during the last two years, I know that the Geelong Society have imported about 700. Expirees or persons with a conditional pardons we believe they are all expirees.

Were they all free men when they arrived al Port Phillip. That is to say, they have conditional pardons enabling them to roam about these colonies ? No, I believe they are all free men who have served their time out, and who have received free pardons without any restrictions.

As a class, how have they turned out ; do you think them a good description of immigrants ? They are great vagabonds, a wretched class of men, the refuse of Van Diemen's Land.

Are they people that have learned any useful occupation in Van Diemen's Land ; have they learned to shear and to tend sheep ? They have learned bush life, shearing and splitting, and so forth, but they have learned a good deal of crime also.

You consider them a very bad class of immigrants ? The very worst we ever had, though, certainly, they are better than nothing.

And is it upon that principle they have been imported ? Yes, merely to keep down the exorbitant price of labor.

By Dr. Bland. — Do they understand sheep? They have been accustomed to sheep, and bush work generally, but are of no use as house servants.

By the Chairman. — Have you had any experience of Pentonville exiles. A great many of them have been employed by settlers with whom I am acquainted.

What do you think of them ? I think they are the best class of men we ever had, and, as a body, superior to the class of immigrants sent from home. They are a young and hardy class of men, ranging from eighteen to twenty-eight or thirty years of age.

And are they useful? They are very useful, and there it a degree of civility about them that you do not find among the Van Diemen's Land expirees.

How many Petionville exiles have been landed at Port Phillip ? About 280 altogether ; there were twenty-one who came with Messrs. Yaldwin and Black, they were capital house servants.

By Mr. Robinson — Have any of these Pentonville exiles committed crimes since they have come to Port Phillip ? I have heard of but few instances.

By Mr. Windeyer. — Are there many of these exiles above twenty years of age? Yes, the average age I should say is about twenty-three or twenty-four.

By the Chairman. — Have you had any experience of the Parkhurst Boys? No we have never had any sent to Port Phillip.

By Mr. Foster.— Are you aware that there are associations in Port Phillip for importing labor from Van Diemen's Land? I know of four.

By the Chairman — Have you employed any expirees from this colony, persons who have served their sentences here? Yes; I have employed a great number of what we call " Sydney Old Hands " Are they better or worse than the Van Demonian refuse yon talk of? I should say the Vandemonian refuse are worse a great deal than those from New South Wales.

By Mr Foster — Do you speak of their morals or as their capabilities as bush-men? I speak as regards their general usefulness.

By the Chairman — Does it come within your knowledge that many crimes have been committed by the expirees from Van Diemen's Land since their first arrival in your district ? Since their first arrival there have been loud outcries in and about the town of their committing depredation and crime.

By Mr Windeyer — Has not the police in the town of Melbourne been obliged to be doubled ? It has I believe been doubled whether on account of that or not I do not know.

By Mr Dangar — What have been the wages of the Pentonville men ? They were kept by the Government until they were offered a fair rate of wages, from £17 to £23 a-year, and if they refused that, they were, I believe, turned adrift.

By the Chairman — If a large number of convicts were introduced into Port Phillip would they meet with employment among the settlers? Immediately.

You think there would be no difficulty in dispersing these people, and employ-ng them away from towns ? Not the slightest ; several thousands might be employed in the country.

Might they be dispersed through the country in that way ? Immediately on their arrival.

By Dr. Bland — You state that the police have been obliged to be increased since the arrival of these persons from Van Diemen's Land ? I believe they have been increased of late.

By the Chairman. — Do you know whether there is an excess of this labor in Van Diemen's Land ? I have heard Vandemonians say that there was.

Do not a great number of these expirees come over to Port Phillip of their own accord ? Yes, a number have done so ; such as could raise £1 a-head to pay their passage.

By Mr. Foster. — You expect a large influx of this description of persons ? Yes, arrangements have been made to continue their importation, but as a matter of necessity alone.

A year after Edmunds arrival, his father died on 28th November, 1847. There was an article in the paper about what happened to him. I wonder if Edmund ever knew about his death?

> *Salisbury Infirmary.*—At a meeting of the Weekly Committee of Governors, held on Saturday, the 4th inst., the case of George Perry, who died in this Infirmary on the previous Sunday, having been brought under the notice of the Committee, it appeared that the patient was admitted on the 13th of November, with a tumour in the leg; that on Friday, the 19th ult., a consultation of all the physicians and surgeons was held, at which it was by a *majority* resolved that the tumour should be extracted; that the operation was accordingly commenced on the following Monday by the surgeon under whose care the patient was, in the presence of one of the consulting surgeons and three other of the medical officers of the establishment; that in the course of operation it was found to be of such a nature as to render immediate amputation necessary, and in this opinion the medical officers with the consulting surgeon were *unanimous.* The amputation was accordingly effected, and no unfavourable symptoms appeared until six days after the operation. It was resolved, " That the Committee are of opinion, that there was no want either of skill or attention on the part of the operating surgeon; but it would have been more satisfactory if the patient had been previously informed of the possibility that the operation of extracting the tumour might render the amputation of the limb necessary." Carried unanimously.

With Edmund transported to Australia and George dead, I wondered what had happened to his mother, Elizabeth and the other children.

The 1851 census lists Elizabeth and the three youngest children, Mary (aged 14), Elizabeth (11) and Martha (aged 8) living on the street as paupers!

In the 1861 census Elizabeth has accommodation and Martha is still with her, and she is working as a carter.

In 1878, Elizabeth died. She was 77 years old and was buried at Nunton, Wiltshire with her husband George.

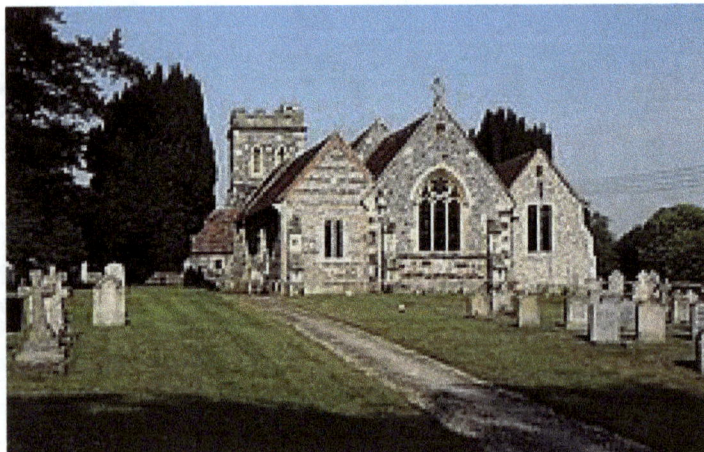

Ellen Gormley

I'm not sure where Edmund lived or worked when he first arrived in Australia, but he must have been in the Richmond area because he married Ellen Gormley on 26th August 1850 in the St Francis Church.

St Francis' Church is a Roman Catholic church, located on the corner of Lonsdale and Elizabeth streets, Melbourne, Victoria, Australia. It is the oldest Catholic church in Victoria. The main body of the church is one of very few buildings in central Melbourne which was built before the Victorian gold rush of 1851.

Ellen Gormley was born in 1831 in Strabane, in the Irish County of Tyrone. Her father was Michael and her mother may have been Cecilia, however I can't prove that. I don't have any other information about her family at this stage.

Here is an early picture of Strabane.

There was a terrible famine in Ireland from around 1845 when Ellen was an adolescent. This was a time of great hunger. People were left destitute and many died. Ellen found herself in the Strabane Workhouse. I haven't been able to find out how long she was there for or whether others from her family were there, however, one of the rules is that all family members had to enter at the same time, so that the landlords could clear out the tenancies.

Strabane Workhouse

The Workhouse was opened in 1841 at a cost of £8,240. It was built to house a maximum capacity of 800 inmates.

Workhouses were established to provide for people who were too poor, sick or elderly to care for themselves. People voluntarily admitted themselves, usually out of desperation. The workhouses weren't set up to be attractive options, rather they were a last resort for people feeling hopeless. They were frightened but as food became even more scarce, parents had to make the decision that it was better to be inside than outside. Outside there was no work, no shelter and for many, no food.

There was a process for admittance. Unless single, an entire family was only allowed in, if the man wanted to leave, the entire family had to leave. An initial interview would take place to establish the family's circumstances and if they were deemed destitute enough they would be approved as Probationary Inmates. They would be stripped, bathed and issued a uniform. They were assessed medically, and if ill would be placed into a sick ward. All their clothes were disinfected and placed into storage with their other possessions, ready for when they left. The children had their hair cut short.

The families were divided into different buildings. The women and children under 2 were allowed to stay together in one building with older children and men being housed separately. There was no communication allowed between the family members. If caught they would be punished.

Everyone entering the workhouse had to obey the strict rules which included working each day except Sunday. Work included cooking, washing, scrubbing, breaking stones, rearing pigs, gardening, repairing the building or picking oakum.

Once inside, your life was controlled by a bell and a strict routine. A typical day was to rise when the bell was rung at 6am; breakfast at 6.30am, work until 12 noon, lunch break and then work until 6pm. Supper was served at 7pm, with final lights out at 8pm. A roll call was carried out each morning. Meal breaks were in the communal dining room and held in silence.

Children attended school a few hours a day and were taught reading, writing and arithmetic.

An inmate's only possessions were his/her uniform, mattress (a sack filled with straw) and a thin blanket. Toilet facilities were primitive to say the least. Once a week the inmates were bathed and the men shaved.

An adult in the workhouse in 1845 had three meals per day, breakfast, dinner and supper. Breakfast consisted usually of six to eight ounces of oatmeal served in a stirabout form with either sweet or sour milk. Potatoes, meat and vegetables were for dinner. However, the amount of meat was very small being no more than 4 ounces per week. Vegetables very often in the form of soup were grown in the workhouse and not always available. Supper was bread and tea. During the worst of the famine potatoes were in very short supply and replaced with Indian meal from America. (This was coarse meal usually fed to animals).

Women in a Victorian era Workhouse

Inmates were not allowed to leave the workhouse without permission. If they did so and were caught, they would be charged with stealing (the workhouse uniform).

I wonder how Ellen would describe her time at Strabane Workhouse? I'm sure she would rather not have lived and experienced that life.

Ellen was selected as part of the Female Famine Orphan Scheme to emigrate to Australia. So now we have Ellen embarking on a new adventure in her life. I wonder how she coped with everything. Her life up till now had been harsh. She had lived through a famine, through poverty, through losing her family who were either dead or else she hadn't been allowed to have anything to do with them in the workhouse. She had experienced the workhouse with all its rules and regulations. She had survived to 19 and now she off to Australia. Had Ellen any say in this? Did she want to go? Was she scared or excited?

When people discharged from the workhouses they were given back the belongings including the clothes they arrived in, and gave back their uniforms. We don't know how long Ellen was an inmate, so I wonder did her clothes and shoes still fit her? Did the Strabane Workhouse treat Ellen and her ten companions the same as the girls who joined our 10 travellers, from the Omagh Workhouse. Below is an article about them:

OMAGH UNION.—DEPORTATION OF PAUPERS.— The guardians of this union have sent nineteen orphan girls from the workhouse, this week, provided with a suitable outfit, as emigrants to Australia, the government providing them with a free passage from Plymouth, to which their expenses are defrayed by the union. The girls on leaving presented an exceedingly clean and respectable appearance. being comfortably, neatly, and rather picturesquely dressed in tartan cloaks and straw bonnets, reflecting much credit on the master and matron, Mr. and Mrs. Klophel, who superintended the necessary preparations. Four orphan girls from the Gortin workhouse were also sent at same time, provided with a similar outfit. The girls will have the advantage of a fair start in life, to push their fortunes in Australia. We could not help thinking. on witnessing the comfortable provision made for them, that Ireland is the only country in the world exhibiting the strange anomaly of the lot of the indigent, idle pauper, being made infinitely superior to that of the industrious labourer. It is not strange that under such circumstances demoralisation grows apace.

A Female Orphan Scheme to transport girls from the workhouses of Ireland to Australia – known as the 'Earl Grey Scheme' – was devised by Secretary of State for the Colonies, Henry Grey, 3rd Earl Grey, during the Great Famine, 1845-52. Although Irish orphan girls had been transported to Australia earlier in the nineteenth century, Grey's scheme intended to reduce the amount of girls in workhouses; but it would also benefit Australia as it would decrease the gender imbalance which had become problematic in the colonies.

One of the rationales for shipping poor, orphaned girls to the Australian colonies was to address a problem of gender imbalance. In the decade prior to the beginning of the Earl Grey scheme, New South Wales had a particularly problematic imbalance with the majority of the 77,000 strong population being male. The previous schemes attempting to bring girls from Ireland to Australia had proved fruitless with a lack of organisation by the colonists resulting in many of these women becoming homeless with many turning to prostitution. Even though schemes like this had already proven to be quite unsuccessful, there were conflicting ideas shown in the press at the potential of several more thousand females arriving to Australia.

The South Australian newspaper based in Adelaide stated in September 1848 that an 'erroneous impression' had been made of Irish orphan immigration to Australia. It was expected that as the girls came from the workhouses they would have a decent standard of training for work and settle well as loyal servants. It was also noted that the architects of the scheme had stated that 'fair wages shall be paid by the employers, according to the current rate prevailing in the district' with a deduction for clothing and expenses. However, the unnamed author of the report objected to the rate of wages – £5 per annum for girls aged 14 going up to £11 per annum by age 18 and £8 per annum for boys of 14, going up to £14 for 18 year olds. This would put these children on higher wages than servants in England. Moreover, the word from New South Wales was that servants who had previously been on a low diet were expensive!

There were 20 ships, with over 4,000 girls, that carried the orphans to Australia and on 3rd October, 1849, "The Derwent" sailed from Plymouth with Ellen on board. There were 10 other girls from the Strabane workhouse that went with her:

ARBUCKLE, Ann, 18	ARBUCKLE, Mary, 23
ARBUCKLE, Sarah, 16	PATTERSON, Mary, 16
SHARKEY, Sarah J. , 17	TAYLOR, Isabella, 16
TAYLOR, Mary Jane, 19	WASON, Jane, 16
WOOLAGHAN OR OULAGHAN, Elizabeth, 17	WOOLAGHAN OR OULAGHAN, Martha, 20

Ellen arrived 25 February, 1850 into Port Phillip Bay. That time of the year, the weather would have been warm, and coming from the Irish winter to the Australian summer must have been an interesting experience.

> The 'Derwent,' proceeds to Portland, where she will be loaded by S. G. Henty, Esq. for London.
>
> The 'River Chief' put in here yesterday on her way to California, having sailed from Melbourne on the 6th instant. She was obliged to touch at this harbour for supplies of water and provisions. *New Zealander*, January 26.
>
> The 'Derwent' brings 140 single females under 20 years of age, 7 married couples and 4 infants; one birth took place during the passage, but not any deaths. She spoke no vessels during the voyage.
>
> We observe by the Adelaide papers that Captain Lewis Tobias Douglas, master of the barque 'Douglas,' now in port, was fined in the Resident Magistrate's Court the sum of five pounds being

An advertisement was placed in the newspapers, letting prospective employers know of their availability. Ellen was lucky to have found a position, as a house servant, with Joseph L'estrange. She was paid 12 pounds for the six month contract, which was one pound above the going rate. I wonder how she was treated? Did she like her new job and her new employers?

> **Orphans per "Derwent."**
>
> NOTICE is hereby given that the Female Orphans per "Derwent," are open for hire at the Depôt, between the hours of 11 o'clock a.m., and 3 o'clock p.m.
>
> By order of the
> Board of Guardians.
> **HENRY GINN,**
> Hon. Secretary.
>
> Melbourne,
> 6th March, 1850.   [5191

There was an article in the Advocate newspaper on 18 March, 1920 about Joseph L'Estrange and his home. Here is a part of the article:

"Of the many noble edifices that crown the hills east of the city of Melbourne, and give striking evidence of the activity and generosity of the Catholic people, the Church of St. Ignatius holds pride of place. Richmondites regard their magnificent church with a particular veneration, and as Richmondites are to be found all over the continent, the golden jubilee of St. Ignatius' is an event that is exciting widespread interest RISE OF A FLOURISHING PARISH. At the present time, Richmond lays claim to having the largest church, not a Cathedral, in Australia. In the early fifties, however, people living where Richmond is now were obliged to go to St. Francis' Church to hear Mass. In consequence of the distance, many people (thus the Very Rev. Fr. Ryan, S.J., in his "Memoirs of the Richmond Mission") could not assist at Mass, and Mr. L'Estrange, solicitor, in the name of the Catholic residents, made an appeal to the Most Rev. James Alipius Goold, O.S.A., Bishop of Melbourne, to grant them that consolation. The Bishop yielded to their request, and the Rev. James J. Madden was appointed to take charge of the district.

In the early part of 1853, a little before Easter, Fr. Madden took up his residence in Richmond in the house of Mr. L'Estrange. Mr. L'Estrange was born in Kingstown, near Dublin, in 1811. He came to Australia in 1839, and, after spending some time in Sydney, he arrived in Melbourne in 1840. He was Chief Clerk in the Crown Law department from its Inception for a period of forty years, during -which time he was for two years Acting Crown Solicitor, in 1846 he built a substantial residence of basalt stone in a nine-acre paddock situated between what are now called Highett-street Bromham-place, and Ross-street. He named the house "Erindale." It was the second house erected in the district. It was in "Erindale" that the first Mass in Richmond was celebrated. Among those present on that memorable occasion were Messrs. Joseph L'Estrange, James Madden, Michael Brickley, Anthony Carroll, Patrick Madden, Jeremiah Maher, William Ryan, Jeremiah Bowe, John Mahony, David Doherty, James Brandon, James Malin, Michael Sheedy, Mrs. Maher, Mrs. D. Madden, Mrs. Heaton, and Mrs.Horan. For some considerable time Mass was celebrated on Sundays in the house of Mr. L'Estrange. As, however, this house was rather remote from many of the parishioners, and afforded insufficient accommodation to the increasing congregation, a move was made for a time to Abinger-street, and soon afterwards a house built by Mr. Richard Flitzgerald in Charlotte-Street was purchased for a presbytery.

The tabernacle in which the Blessed Sacrament was preserved for years in the L'Estrange family, and has been given by Mrs. L'Estrange to the Jesuit Fathers. A brass tablet is now affixed to it, bearing the following inscription:— "This is the Tabernacle in which the Blessed Sacrament was reserved in the house of Mr. Joseph L'Estrange in 1853, before St. James' Church was built on Bridge-road.

Above is a picture of "Erindale"

Below is picture of Joseph L'Estrange taken 1n 1868

Ellen met and married Edmund as soon as her contract was ended. He must have been living very close by, for the two to have met, fallen in love and marry so quickly.

I have continued their story together in the next chapter.

Ellen died in November, 1905. From the articles in the newspapers, it seems she had been living in a little cottage near Mariners Reef at the time. Mariners Reef was a mine site area, close to Maryborough, Victoria.   The report says her son found her, fully dressed, on the sofa. Sounds peaceful.

LONELY DEATH.

Maryborough, 6th November.

Mrs. Perry, aged about 74 years, was found dead in her hut near Maryborough to-day. Her son left her this morning, when she appeared to be in her usual state of health. On returning in the afternoon he found her dead, and reported the matter to the police. There are no suspicious circumstances.

Ellen Gormley

How sad she had such a lonely death.

Bendigo Advertiser
7 November, 1905

The Age

7 November, 1905

ELDERLY WOMAN FOUND DEAD.
MARYBOROUGH, Monday.

A woman named Perry, aged 74, was found dead in her house to-day. She lived in a little cottage near Mariner's Reef, and was in her usual state of health this morning at 8.30 o'clock, but upon her son visiting the place early this afternoon he found her lying dead, fully dressed, on the sofa. The matter was reported to Sergeant Beresford, who deputed Constable Horn to make inquiries. He reported that there were no suspicious circumstances in the case. The matter was reported to the coroner.

Edmund and Ellen Perry

Ellen's contract of employment ended and she immediately married Edmund Perry on 26th August, 1950 in the St Francis Church in Melbourne.

Edmund and Ellen had twins on 28th June 1851 when they were living in Richmond. Their names were George (d 24 July, 1926) and Margaret (d 9 June 1926).

Melbourne at this time was a bustle of activity. There was a lot of building going on as the City started to develop. There would have been a lot of work around for Edmund.

Here is a picture of Melbourne in the 1850's.

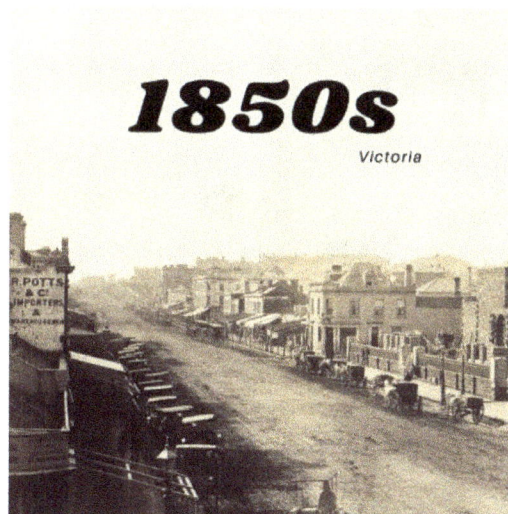

There was a huge gold rush in the United States and the newspapers were reporting all the latest from there. There was geological research in Victoria going on, to find the natural resources including gold. I'd say that there was a lot of excitement building on the hopes of discovering it. Edmund and Ellen, would no doubt have been caught up with this hype.

When, in 1852 gold was discovered in Central Victoria, Edmund and Ellen moved and settled in the Maryborough area.

I love this picture of a pub in Maryborough in 1856.

Being amongst the first settlers in the region, they watched as the place was transformed over the next few decades. From being a very sparsely populated area to a small city, they watched it all.

Here is picture taken in the 1890's of Maryborough.

Life on the goldfields was probably not easy for Edmund and Ellen. They probably lived in a tent or a shanty in the early years. I can only imagine the struggles they had, trying to eke out a living all while producing a large family.

When Edmund and Ellen moved to Maryborough it was more a farming area. Although some gold had been discovered, the Gold Rush hadn't yet begun in full earnest. I assume Edmund found work on a farm, but I have no records for this. He more than likely would have found work in the gold mines or independently prospected later.

Edmund and Ellen had 9 more children:
Mary Jane Perry 1855-after 1869
William Perry 1857–1918
Edward Perry 1859–1860
James Perry 1861–1861|
Elizabeth Margaret Perry 1865–1937
Ellen Perry 1866–1953
Charles Perry 1869–1947
Edmond Perry 1871–1890
Sarah Ann Perry 1874–1900

Edmund was 49 years old when Sarah was born and Ellen was 43. As you see from the above, Edward (buried at Majorca Cemetery) and James both died as infants. Edmond died at age 19.

There weren't a lot of women in the area and I wonder, how did Ellen manage with the young children? Being a young mother without family support can be hard! Where were they living? Were they able to rent a house or did they live in a hut that Edmund built?

.In 1860 their son Edward who was around 1 died and was buried in Majorca. This leads me to think they were living there at the time.

There were two schools in Majorca. The first Majorca school opened as a common school in 1864. The school wasn't recognised by the Board of Education, yet it remained open without aid. It is not known when this school closed. The first head teacher was Frederick O'Connell Lane, who taught 80 students. A second school listed by the Board of Education was Majorca Common School (No. 764.) The Board approved a grant for 75 pounds to build the school in 1867. However, because of delays the school didn't open until 1868. The first head teacher was George Wilmot.

Schools in Victoria were not made compulsory until 1872. On 23 August, 1881, Edmund was fined for not sending his son Edmund, who would have been 9 or 10 years old, to school. He claimed that the boy played truant.

Maryborough, Hospital.

Edmund died in 1896 in the Maryborough Hospital. Here is an early picture of the hospital.

I found these fantastic articles in The Weekly Times, published 29 September, 1928 about the history of Maryborough, which will give us an insight into what it was like in the area. The articles illustrate the cultural development and how important progress was to the area.

Weekly Times (Melbourne, Vic. : 1869 - 1954), Saturday 29 September 1928, page 12

VICTORIA'S COUNTRY TOWNS
Their Rise and Development
No. 15. — History of Maryborough

By FRANK WHITCOMBE

THE call of Maryborough is not wholly accounted for by its origin 'midst the idyllic scenes of Simson's Run, in a region rich in undiscovered nuggets, set in preparation for the drama of the early fifties, but in the aura of romance surrounding the history of those protagonists occupying the stage when Maryborough was in the making; whose roles are remembered by surviving pioneers or recorded in the book of the play. The red-shirted digger; the desperado, the truth of whose existence was stranger than any fiction dealing with it; the adventurous trader who multiplied or lost his all, and ever at his personal risk; have all played their parts in the building up of modern Maryborough — a town that has found itself, and looks forward with sober confidence to a continuation of prosperity.

Foremost in point of time was D. C. Simson, who held the land in all the confident simplicity of his squatterdom, with an eye for area and sheep that innocently increased in number and fed amongst unsuspected gold; and in utter ignorance of the riches which he was daily treading underfoot. D. C. Simson from all accounts, in 1837 overlanded his mobs of sheep, cattle and horses from Monaro, N.S.W., via the Snowy River, crossing when the water was low above Orbost, eventually reaching Charlotte Plains, named after his wife, and pitching his homestead seven miles from Maryborough. The station covered 100,000 acres, bounded by the low hills since known as Simson's Ranges and watered by the Loddon and Deep Creek. This run extended towards Bendigo, Dunolly and Maldon, and included the present township of Maryborough.

From the memoirs of his son, J. C. Simson, born at the homestead in 1840, a bullock driver in 1842 sold his father a nugget which he stated he had picked up on the run at Daisy Hill (Talbot), six miles from Maryborough, but Mr Simson, senr., was sceptical of its place of origin, not withstanding that six years later in 1848, there were 10,000 diggers on good gold frantically turning over his ground.

Two years after the advent of D. C. Simson on the Loddon, other land seekers followed, and effected a settlement at Carisbrook, which soon became the pastoral and social centre of the surrounding countryside. Race meetings were held there, and at one D. C. Simson's Flying Buck, bred at Charlotte Plains, afterwards winner of the first Champion Stakes run at Flemington, carried off the highest honors.

The First Nugget It has never been satisfactorily settled as to how, when or where the discovery was made. It remains a matter of surprise that the bullock driver, after picking up a nugget, should not have found others in a district literally strewn with them at slight depth beneath the surface.

A party of diggers returning from Bendigo in 1854, casually prospecting as they Travelled along, are generally credited with finding gold in Mary borough itself at the south end of the present High street; whilst a third person, one Rice, claimed to have un-earthed gold on his road from Avoca, and applied somewhat belatedly after, the time had run out for the Government reward.

Rumors were followed by the inevitable rush, on the site of the present town. High street was pegged out with a mile and a half of canvas tents, following the rich alluvial lead. A demand for a defined township became insistent, and Mary-borough was surveyed by W. A. Taylor in April, 1855. followed by Crown land sales in October, 1856.

The principal thoroughfares, highly reminiscent of the Crimean War. were named Inkerman. Varna. Nolan. Florence. Nightingale and Wyndham streets. The town itself, according to a framed letter from Gold Commissioner Daly, shown the writer by Mr Henry Neville Phillips, C.R.. town clerk owed its name to 'the Commissioner's birthplace in Ireland. With the discovery of fresh gold deposits, Maryborough was created a borough in 1857. the first civic fathers being Crs. D. Taylor. D. K. Campbell, Roberts. Garland, Levy. Fowler and A. M. Landress, and the secretarial duties were entrusted to J. C. Hooper. Municipal Honors Prior to 1857 Maryborough had been governed by a road board, and as far back as December. 1855. agitation had been rife for advanced municipal status.

As the result of a petition to the Colonial Secretary, signed on 28th July, 1856, by Messrs. De Pass and Co. (merchants). Thomas Decker (produce dealer). F. Fitzpatrick (publican). Fred Ogle (chemist). Frank Jones (tent maker), R. Souter (restaurant keeper). Thomas Andrews. Alexander S. Palmer. Joseph Davis. Hugh McMillan, Walter Smith. Wm. B. Collyns. Thomas Hinds, and others, Maryborough became a borough. T. Gardner, who during Cr. Taylor's mayoralty, was town clerk, was subsequently town clerk for some years of the City of Richmond.

The present area of the borough is 5760 acres, with a population of 5040. distributed in 1150 dwellings, and with a revenue of £10.000. The present Mayor is Cr. John A. Roberts, with Crs. J. S. Stevens. Charles Waters. James Elliott. J.P.. John R. Bryant. Samuel Poole. Robert W. Laidlaw. J.P., Henry E. Williams, J.P., John Lean. J.P., and Henry Neville Phillips, C.H., .JP., who has filled the position of town clerk for 40 years.

Former occupants of the Mayoral chair were: Crs. Alex. McLandress. D. K. Campbell. D. Taylor (thrice), D. Christian. E. Legge. A. Lowenstein (thrice), E. Harkness, T. Casey (seven times), H. R. Wharton, W. M. Page. G. Knight, G. Carrick. R. B. Stamp. Hon. A. R. Outtrim (twice). J. Logan (thrice). F. J. Field (thrice). J. H. Gearing. J. C. F. Uldrich, J. P. Kennedy, E. Fox Pollard (twice). H. E. Williams (twice), A. J. Smith. Robert Hubble (twice). John McLennan. T. C. Miers, A. E. M. Diggings (twice), J. R. Green. J. J. Lewcas, O. H. McDonah. Ike Solomon, H. R. Richardson, George Frost. J. R. Lamb, James Eliott. .T. H. Pascoe. John Lean. C. S. Taylor. R. W. Laidlaw.

Agriculture Goes Ahead Land values are rising, as an instance will demonstrate. In 1916 allotments having 66ft. frontage with a depth of 120ft;. up in the gaol reserve, sold at £10 a block, and have recently changed hands at up to £140: and whereas in 1915 houses were being sold and carted away at from £45 to £50 each, they now fetch from £400 to £500. The average prices for good country within the districts of Carlsbrook, Moolort, Eddington. Wareek. Bung Bong, are from £10 to £14, and up to £20 an acre; one farm of 110 acres, lucerne soil, being recently sold for £29 an acre. On account of the ease with which lucerne can be grown in the district, fat lamb raising is be coming increasingly popular amongst farmers; who also hold the opinion that the best oaten hay in Victoria hails from Moolort.   There is a fair amount of good wheat land about four or five miles out from Maryborough.   The agricultural area has been extended 300 per cent, during the last 10 years, stud cattle are being judiciously imported, the lambing percentage is most satisfactory, many dairies carry 350 cows, of pigs are reared, and poultry farming is receiving greatly increased attention.

Maryborough has been represented in the House by several members of great outstanding ability and penetrating personality; such men as A. R. Outtrim. Minister for Mines: Duncan Gillies, Premier; B. C. Aspinall, eminent lawyer, capable of convulsing Bench, Bar and Parliament with anecdotal sallies that swayed jurymen and wheedled politicians; David Blair, brilliant man of letters; "Dick" Ireland, Attorney-General by sheer force of forensic geniality; Dr. Evans, journalist of repute, and receiver of port folio. All men of mark and Maryborough!

Notable Men Maryborough in its heyday attracted such men as E. G. FitzGibbon. C.M.G.. the White Knight, who later exchanged the lure of the pick for the emoluments of office in Melbourne; Henry Hoylen Hayter, C.M.G., the eminent statistician; Chief Police Commissioner Chomley; and Sir Julius Vogel. who made the Maryborough and Dunolly Advertiser a stepping stone to the Premiership of the New Zealand Government; where he was placed upon a pedestal as the marvellous financier of the "seventies," who wheedled £10,000.000 by way of a loan out of the fiscal magnates of London.

The Advertiser was the nursery of others who acquired fame in after life, notably Mr. Robinson, the police magistrate, who gravitated to New Zealand also; and Mr. E. J. Bateman. who became proprietor of the Talbot Leader, and then at Ballarat in partnership with Mr Robert Clark established the Ballarat Courier. Dr. Quick was at one time engaged on the Advertiser. Mr F. Macoboy. uncle of Chief Justice Sir John Madden, was County Court judge; Mr. G. Augustus Thompson presided at the Warden's Court: Dr. F. M. Laidman was the Coroner, and worked on the diggings as a miner before starting practice in Melbourne. He died in 1879. Huntley Hoskins was a solicitor In the digging days; and Mr F. Call, police magistrate. The latter was a conscientious man. popular and keen to detect any attempted sharp practice or quibbling on the part of a litigant; and, yet After his promotion to Melbourne and when sitting on the bench in the old police court, adjoining the Town Hall, In Swanston street, he fell to a man with a ladder, who apologising for intruding during hearing of evidence against a prisoner, charged with larceny, proceeded to wind up the courtroom clock, and then with a gesture of annoyance, said he was sorry to keep his Worship interrupted, but he would have to take the clock away to repair it. He took it away without demur, and pledged it with a complaisant pawnbroker. ;

The Pioneers Included in the cast of those who have occupied the crowded stage and have spoken their parts, and helped to leave an impress on the story of the town, were: — William Williams, who arrived from Shropshire in 1852. and followed the gold mining until his death. One of his sons, Cr. H. E. Williams, a large property owner in the town and district, started business in 18S6 as a produce merchant, and has been a councillor since 1880, and has several times occupied the Mayoral chair: been 32 years on the committee of the District Hospital, of which he was treasurer for 16 years, president of the Show, and president for 10 consecutive years of the Swimming Club, besides being a justice of the Peace and the deputy Coroner.

James Hugh Gearing, twice Mayor of Maryborough, born in Brompton, England, in 1821, came out in the ship Semaphore to Melbourne in October, 1852, after serving his time at the printing trade. Following the gold rushes he returned to work at his trade in Melbourne; and In 1885 established a printing business in Maryborough, in partnership with E. H. Nutliall. and then published the Fiery Creek Advertiser, and a paper at Dunolly. In 1873 he brought out the Maryborough Standard. He was an active member of the Anglican churches in Maryborough and Majorca, vice-president of the District Hospital, treasurer of the Maryborough Garrick Club, and volunteer fire brigade, member of the Volunteer Corps, and Literary and Mechanics' Institute. In 18S6 he was returned unopposed to the Borough Council, and took a keen Interest' in public matters. He helped in the formation of the local gap company, and was president of the Maryborough Bowling Club.

The best known man in Maryborough in the 60 s, 70 s and 80 s, was John Spellman. the bellringer. Daniel Plucke. a ship's captain, in 1854 transferred his affections from the deep blue sea to the gold rush at Alma, four miles from the Simson's diggings, and in 1856 opened an iron mongery business in High street, still successfully carried on by his sons. Bernard King, who had a tailor's shop in the early days, extended his business to Collins street, Melbourne F. R. Beaity was one of the first bonifaces of the old Bull and Mouth Hotel. James Logan. Mayor of Maryborough in 18S9 and again in 1908, , was born in Stirlingshire in 1829, and landed in Victoria in 1853, and after mining at Tarrengower and Simson's Ranges, commenced storekeeping at the Alma, where he purchased and farmed 500 acres. In 1879 he settled in Maryborough, and carried on business as general storekeeper and auctioneer for a quarter of a century. The second generation loyally carry on the Alma homestead.

First Business Ventures Daniel Taylor, a native of Perth shire, arriving in Melbourne in 1852. after a round of the rushes reached Maryborough in 1854; and for several years managed the store of C. Steel, eventually purchasing it. He was a member of the Borough Council from its gazettal in 1857, and attained to Mayoral honors in 1861, 1864 and 1874, and was the original chairman of the Maryborough water scheme. James TV. Butler, born in London, visited the Forest Creek, Bendigo. and Simson's Ranges goldfields in 1852. and opened a general store under canvas in the present High street.

Maryborough, before any houses were thought of and when bullock teams took 14 days for the trip from Melbourne. Three sons and two daughters settled on the land at Moolort and Joyce's Creek. One of the family. Mr Reg. Boiler, carries on the Bull and Mouth Hotel, and prior to entering into possession was in the police force for 20 years and 5 months; during which time he captured the Pearce Brothers in connection with the murder of Mr Davidson in Tennyson street. St. Kilda. Alexander Lowenstein, born in 1830 at Dantzig, Germany, arrived in Melbourne in 1854. and journeyed on foot to Forest Creek, making his way to Maryborough, the Alma and other diggings. in 1858 he opened a tobacconist's business with headquarters at Maryborough, and developed into a mining manager, including such mines as the Magnum Bonum Extended, the Band of Hope. Duke and Timor, and Queen and Count Bismarck. He was Mayor of Maryborough for four terms, and was presented with a silver trowel when he laid the foundation stone of the new town hall in 1887. Thomas Grendy was landlord of the Bristol Arms Hotel, near Bristol Hil known as the Hill of Gold, and on the slopes of which The old cemetery was located.

Wm. Rhodes Camp Hotel was so called because it was on the main camping ground, and the police camp was opposite his house in what is now Royal Park. Benjamin Wiillan. one of the early birds, kept the Talbot Family Hotel. Dr. Dunn, the first medical officer of the District Hospital, occupied the position for 49 years, | W. C. Wilson. at one time connected with Melvor's Hotel, afterwards bought an interest in Scott's Hotel, Melbourne. Thomas II. Sears, who succeeded Wilson, left Maryborough to take over Rennison's Hotel at Schnapper Point in the seventies, returning to occupy the old Bull and Mouth.

The Father of Maryborough Tomas Casey, for over 30 years captain of the local volunteer fire brigade, formed in 1861, on several occasions filled the Presidential chair of the Country Fire Brigades' Board, and earned a State wide reputation. He was Mayor for several terms between 1869 and 1905, and was known as "the Father of Maryborough," an undertaker by profession and fireman by natural impulse.

Mr M F. Ogle's chemist's shop and dispensary occupies the very site in High street where his father in 1854 pitched tent, and opened his medicine chest for the cure of current distempers. His memories as a boy of the rowdy picturesqueness of his surroundings, and of the clashes between honest representative diggers and the lawless gangs of Derwenters and Sydneysiders are vividly interesting.

Other very early residents of Mary-borough were:— D. W. Virtue, auctioneer; D. K. Campbell and Collyns and Co., merchants; Foote and Heather, warehousemen; Kersley and Lord, warehousemen. Lord was lost In the London, crossing the Bay of Biscay, in the year 1866; a fellow passenger with G. V. Brooke, the famous Shakespearean actor. Levi Bros., Valley Store; Reid and Co., coffee merchants; Fowler and Kerr, ironmongers; W. G. McCulloch, storekeeper J. Dalzell, iron founder; H. Hurle, butcher; H. Legge. Commercial Hotel. J. F. Comins, auctioneer; De Pass Bros, and Co.. general store started prior to 1857; F. Schultze. tailor, 1857; R. Sanders, auctioneer, yards site of the present Bull and Mouth Hotel. Alex. McLandress kept the Dundee Boot and Shoe Store in 1857. A. Pettygrove, boots and shoes. Charles Tatlam, glass and china ware; Cameron McCallum and Co., and W. Pender, drapers; Anderson, Harper and Farguson and Peter Virtue and Co., grocers "and wine and spirit merchants; also Ford and Garland; A. G. Hendriques and Co.; John Lawrie; Neil Bruce and Co.. and D. Taylor. W. Edwards; Dicker Bros.; W. Kay and George Stevens were hay and produce dealers in the very early days .

Men of the Fifties.   Men of the Fifties included:-Prendergast and O'Connor, brewers; H. Borland, boot and shoe manufacturer; W. A. Stirling, draper; W. Simson, of the Golden Age Hotel; Ray Clark, butcher; R. W. Farmer and W. D . Ready chemists; John Gardiner, schoolmaster; Cr. J. Hilton, bookseller; Mark Davis, painter; M. Adainson, storekeeper; — Ray, of the Lave and Lei Live Hotel: S. Middleton, baker and publican; Brooks Clay, drapers; Thomas Field, tailor; — Burnie, publican; Cr. F. J. Field, ironmonger t ; thrice Mayor); Houghton and Williams, store-beepers; E. Harvie and W. Beck, bakers; — Salter, Union Hotel; J. Sherman, butcher; H. Earl, storekeeper: W. Allan. Empire Hotel; C. McFarland and NY. Gray, produce dealers; J. Thornbill, grocer. David Elsey was a gardener in the early days, and his sons follow the ....

same profession. Dr. Macdonald, later of Sale, started practice in Maryborough after he landed from Nova Scotia with Mr Simon Fraser. He was father of the present secretary of the Gippsland Hospital (Mr Norman Macdonald), and another son is following in his footsteps in Sale. H. Parnall, a one-time councillor, was a carpenter and wheelwrgiht. T. Taggatt was a carpenter, and timber merchant, and his son, Arthur Taggart owns a furniture business on the same premises. In the early days J. and W. Mathewson. two brothers, were black smiths: and T. Buchanan was a saddler and harness maker. Isaac Harris was a butcher in the 50's, and his sons carry on the same business. James Sutton's grandsons manage the business of produce dealing, which he established in the 50's.

Old man Fuller, as he was familiarly termed, opened brick works in the 50's to build the town. His son still lives in Maryborough. Mr Tremlett, whose grandson is a local hairdresser, was a blacksmith in the 50's. J. Davies was a builder and carpenter in the early days. Cr. Edward Harkness. merchant was Mayor In 1868. Cr. George Knight, who was Mayor in 1880. kept a public house called The Two Brewers, and kept on tap his own home-brewed ales. Wm. Kaye had a grocery business in the gold digging days of the "fifties, which is now carried on by his son-in-law, a brother of the Bishop of Newcastle. L. M. Frilay kept the Shamrock Hotel in the "fifties" in a building now occupied as a grocer's shop by his son in Nolan street. (To be concluded next week)"

There seems to have been a great deal going on and so much progress had been made in such a few short decades. It must have been a very interesting time to be a part of.

I have continued the stories of Edmund and Ellen's children in the next chapters.

The next generations.

In the preceding pages we have watched Edmund and Ellen go from Victorian England and Ireland into a brand new country of Australia. They were amongst the earliest settlers into the Maryborough Victoria area. They worked, and raised a large family, before they died. Edmund was 71 and Ellen was 74. I wonder if they felt that the change in their lives was a good one. From my research I cannot but feel that they were truly fortunate to have made the move, albeit forced upon them.

The following pages will follow their children's and in some cases, their grand and great grand children's lives.

All the information has come from public records so this will only be a glossary of their lives. We don't know their personalities. We don't really know their struggles or their achievements. We can but glimpse the outlines.

I have found the rare photo of some of them and some stories that were written in the newspapers. Sometimes we come across some information that isn't pretty. I have included as much as I can about the people. We may not like some of it, but we don't need to shy away from it. It's all about the human experience in the end.

I have found some great Newspaper articles which talk about the Perry's in our area of interest, around Majorca, Talbot, Maryborough region.

A RUFFIANLY ATTACK.—The *Talbot Leader* says:—" A daring and most dastardly assault and attempted rape was perpetrated last Saturday by a man named Burry on the daughter of Mr Perry, a farmer residing near the Deep Creek, about two miles from Bucknall's station. It appears that Miss Perry, who is about seventeen years of age, was gathering some evergreens to decorate the house with on Christmas Day, and when only a short distance from her father's house, this man Burry, who is a stranger to the family, came up to her, and brutally illused the young lady. In all probability he would have accomplished his purpose had it not been for the strenuous exertions made by Miss Perry to defeat his intention. Being naturally strong, and displaying an amount of courage, seldom found in one of her years, she was enabled to withstand the attacks of this brutal ruffian, until her cries attracted the attention of her father, when the villain made off. Mr Perry immediately gave chase on horseback, but owing to the advantage of a good start, and the difficulty in tracking the culprit, Perry travelled five miles before he overtook him. He was then secured and brought to Majorca, where he is safely lodged for the present. On Wednesday he was brought up at the Police Court, and remanded by De Gouthre, J.P. till Friday, when he was fully committed for trial at the next General Sessions, to be held at Talbot. He did not deny his guilt."

This article talks about a seventeen year old "Miss Perry" and her father.

I think it could be our Margaret Agnes and Edmund.

This was found in the Bendigo Advertiser 3 January, 1866

Dunolly and Bet Bet Express and Country Gladstone Advertiser.

8 September, 1916

Albert Richard Cornwill

in high honor and strong affection. Another son and brother, Signaller Charles G-me, is now at the front.

A young man, 23 years of age, named Albert Cornwill, belonging to Majorca, but who had been working near Dunolly for Mr Rhode Khan, was admitted on Wednesday to the Dunolly hospital suffering from injuries received while engaged in grubbing timber. He was working what is known as a " forest devil," when, with a sudden jerk, the handle caught the young man across the stomach. The nature or extent of the injuries, whether there is any internal hurt or not, could not at once be ascertained, but the patient yesterday appeared to be considerably easier.

A SERIES OF ACCIDENTS.
MARYBOROUGH, Tuesday.

A lad named Lucas Leslie Perry, eleven years of age, residing at Majorca, had his hand injured through playing with a dynamite cap. He and another lad were playing with some caps, and Perry had one in his hand when it exploded. The thumb and some of the finger nails were blown off.

Henry Bell, ten years of age, was bird nesting near the Maryborough Brewery this evening, when he fell from a tree, and sustained severe bruising.

A case of ptomaine poisoning occurred to-day at Cockatoo, near Majorca. Two children named William Wallace, three years of age, and Vernon Wallace, two years, wandered from home, and ate a quantity of fungus growth resembling mushrooms. They became very ill, the younger one being in a state of collapse. They were conveyed to the hospital, where they soon recovered after treatment.

John Tranter, aged nine years, residing at Maryborough, was standing near a horse, when the animal lashed out and struck him on the forehead, inflicting a lacerated wound, requiring six stitches.

Left picture

Lucas Leslie Perry.

The Age
19 October, 1904

sine die.

PLAYING WITH DYNAMITE CAPS.
Maryborough, 18th October.

Some dynamite caps were found by some boys on the road in Main-street, Majorca. Lucas Leslie Perry, aged 11 years, placed one of the caps on a stone and struck it with another stone. An explosion followed, and several of the boy's fingers were shattered. He was admitted to the Maryborough Hospital.

Right Picture
Lucas Leslie Perry
Bendigo Advertiser
19 October, 1904

Below
Thomas Percival Lyle Perry
The Argus
29 August 1925

has been left in its natural condition.

Thomas Perry, aged 25 years, a railway employee, who lives at Majorca, was assisting in shunting operations at the Windermere station on Friday, when his foot was caught between the buffers and severely crushed.

COLLAPSE OF RABBIT BURROW

◆

Farm Employee Killed

SEA LAKE, Wednesday. — Herbert Perry, aged 26 years, employed by Mr. Leonard Dickson, farmer, of Nandaly, left the farmhouse yesterday afternoon to dig out rabbits and foxes. Mr. Dickson found him this morning dead in a rabbit burrow. A large quantity of earth had collapsed on him after he had dug most of the deep burrow out. Perry's parents live at Maryborough. On the night before his death Perry was presented with a cup as the best and fairest player in the Nandaly football team.

Herbert William Perry

Son of Edmund Augustus Perry

and

Ada Maud Perry (nee Mason)

The Argus

11 October 1934

Edward George Perry

Son of Edmund August Perry and Ada Maud Perry (nee Mason)

The Argus

9 December, 1940

NO ONE IN BIG CROWD SAW BOY DROWN

MARYBOROUGH, Sunday — Although there was a large crowd of spectators at the official opening of the Maryborough baths yesterday afternoon and there were many swimmers in the water, nobody knew that Edmund George Perry, 7, had fallen into the baths until his fully clothed body was discovered in the water soon after the opening ceremony had ended.

Resuscitation measures were at once begun but they had no effect. An inquest will be held.

The boy's parents live in Maryborough. Four years ago his eldest brother was killed in an accidental fall of earth.

Margaret Agnes Perry

Margaret was born in Richmond, Victoria, in 1851. She was a twin with George.

On 21 September 1869, Margaret married Edward Cornwell. Margaret was 18 at the time and Edward was 20. The marriage certificate states that Edmund Perry is a labourer and Edwards father Edward Cornwill, is a miner. His mothers name was Lucy Lucas. The marriage took place in the Christ Church in Maryborough and was witnessed by John Cornwill, Edwards brother and Mary Jane Perry, Margarets sister.

Margaret and Edward stayed in the area and raised a family. There were 15 children.

Benjamin James Cornwall	1869–1943
William Charles Cornwell	1871–1913
Edward Richard Francis Cornwell	1872–1882
Ellen Lucas Cornwill	1874–1912
Margaret Jane Cornwill	1876–1959
John George Cornwill	1877–1956
Mary Ann Cornwill	1880–1963
Lucy Laura Cornwill	1882–1976
Edith Cornwill	1883–1883
Edward Richard Cornwill	1883–1883
Walter Cornwill	1885–1885
Ethel May Cornwill	1886–1969
Albert Richard Cornwill	1886–1954
Jessie Lucas Cornwill	1889–1890
Florence Ruby Cornwill	1891–1964

Here is a copy of Margaret and Edwards Marriage Certificate.

I found that while researching, the spelling of the family name changed from Cornwall to Cornwell to Cornwill. Apparently, this happened quite a lot in the 1800's. It was probably due to the family member, not being able to read and write, so when they were giving their name, the person writing it down would use their own spelling.

From the 15 children born, 4 were to die in infancy and one died as a child. On the 9th February 1882. Edward Richard Cornwell, (Edmund and Ellen's grandchild) aged 10 accidently drowned in the Bristol Hill dam at Maryborough.

ANOTHER DROWNING ACCIDENT.

A lad named Richard Cornwall was drowned on Thursday evening in the Bristol Hill dam, Maryborough, whither he had gone to bathe with other boys. He got out of his depth, and not being able to swim, immediately sank. The other children gave the alarm, but it was nearly two hours before the body was recovered. It was discovered by Constable O'Connell diving.— *Evening Mail.*

Here is a copy of the inquest report:
It says:

"Magisterial Inquiry

I find that Edward Richard Conrwell was accidentally drowned on the ninth day of February, 1882, whilst bathing in the Bristol Hill dam at Maryborough.

Dated at Maryborough this day 9 February 1882. Signed"

On 6th July, 1888, Edward was fined for not sending one of his children to school.

In 1890 Edward was fined for not sending Albert to school.

On 21st August, 1881? Edward was charged with not sending his son Benjamin to school.

In the Argus on 5th November, 1896 the following notice appeared.

NEW INSOLVENTS.

Edward Cornwill, of Craigie, miner. Liabilities, £71 1s. 9d.; assets, 10s.; deficiency, £70 11s. 9d. Mr. P. Virtue, assignee. Filed at Maryborough.

Evelyn Nightingall, of St. Vincent-place, South Melbourne, married woman. Causes of insolvency—Reduction of monetary allowance made to insolvent, illness of insolvent and members of her family, and medical expenses. Liabilities, £136 8s. 7d.; assets, £72 4s.; deficiency, £64 4s. 7d. Mr. R. E. Jacomb, assignee.

On the 21st July, 1903 Edward was fined 2 shillings and 6pence for his daughter Florence truancy. If he defaulted he could have faced 24 hours imprisonment!

On 18th December, 1903 Edward was taken to court by The Leviathan Reef Goldmines Limited because he owed them 4 pound 1 shilling 11pence.

In July 1904 Edward was fined again for not sending Florence to school.

Edward died on 31st January, 1914. He was 64. He was buried in the Majorca Cemetery.

These 2 notices were placed in the papers.

MR EDWARD CORNWILL.

Mr Edward Cornwill, a resident of Craigie, died yesterday, aged 63 years. The funeral will take place this afternoon, leaving his late residence at 2 o'clock for the Majorca cemetery.

IN MEMORIAM.

CORNWILL.—In loving remembrance of my dear father and husband, Edward Cornwill, who departed this life on 31st day of January, 1914.

He is gone but not forgotten,
Never shall his memory fade,
Sweetest thoughts shall ever linger,
Around our darling father's grave.

—Inserted by his loving daughter and son and wife, Mr and Mrs Harris and Margaret Cornwill.

Margaret died 9th June, 1926 after a long illness in the Maryborough Hospital. She was 75.

The following is Margaret's contribution to the Perry family tree:

Margaret Agnes Perry	1851-1926
married	1869
Edward Cornwell	1849-1914
Children	
Benjamin James Cornwall	1869–1943
married	1899
Eveline Annear	1878-1963
children:	
Doris Irene Cornwill	1899-
married	1927
Harry Trevena Grossman	1899-1965
Frederick Rupert Cornwell	1902-1902
Eric Cornwall	1904-1972
William Charles Cornwell	1871–1913
Married	1891
Emily Harris	1867-1943
Children	
Albert Richard Cornwill	1891–1929
Married	1815
Jessie Cuy	1898-1974
children:	
Dulcie Hazel May Cornwill	1916-1986
Albert Raymond Cornwill	1918-1979
William Charles Cornwill	1920-1998
Walter James Cornwill	1922-1977
Violet Jean Cornwill	1927-2016
James Leslie Cornwill	1892–1985
Married	1916
Blanche Lillian Gibson	1895-1942
Children	
James William Cornwill	1917-1917
Irene Harriet Cornwill	1922-1945
Jean Emma Cornwill	1923-1924
Frederick Bert Cornwill	1926-1989
Married	1943
Lorna Mabel Kelly	1922-2011

Children		
Eileen (Doris) May Brogan	1910-1980	
Married	1933	
Samuel Fraser	1905-1984	
Peter Leslie Brogan (Tunes)	1915-1978	
Married	1935	
Gloria Mena Garlepp	1918-2015	
Children		
Leslie John Tunes	1936-2016	
Lillian Merle Tunes	1937	
Donald Lawrence Tunes	1939	
Janice Marlene Tunes	1940	
Olga May Brogan	1917-1917	
Married	1921	
Ernest Hoy Simpson	1892-1942	

Margaret Cornwill	1895–1947
William Robert Cornwill	1896–1916
Killed in action WW1 Somme, France	
John Raymond Cornwill	1898–1978
Married	1920
Ellen Veronica Howe	1899-1960
Children	
Helen Veronica Cornwill	1920-1993
Thelma Violet Cornwill	1922-1981
Doris Margaret Cornwill	1923-1969
John Walter Cornwill	1926-1993
Leonard Cornwill	1900–1900
Walter Henry Cornwill	1902–1974
Married	1927
Florence Alexandra Cox	1903-1994
Children	
Mavis Cornwill	1930-2005
Graham Cornwill	1939-1939
Margaret Cornwill	1940-1999
Bertie Cornwill	1905–1941
Married	1926
Thelma Olive Greenshaw	1905-1996

Children
Constance Cornwill -1939
Violet Cornwill 1908–1912
Edward Richard Francis Cornwell 1872–1882
Ellen Lucas Cornwill 1874–1912
Married 1892
George William Brown 1874-1932
Children
William Edward Brown 1894-1965
Married 1920
Myrtle Rose Baker 1901-1978
Children
Myrtle Rose Brown 1921-2005
Edna Brown 1922-2007
Harold Brown 1900-1969
Married (cousin) 1922
Alice Marion Hollis Cornwill 1901-1997
children
Dorothy Joan Brown 1924-1983
Leonard George Brown 1903-1978
Married
Doris Ines Mohr 1930
Dorothy Lynette Brown 1931-1988
Margaret Jane Cornwill 1876–1959
Married 1897
James Phillip Judd 1886-1909
Children
John Phillip Judd 1898-1961
Married 1925
Ida Mary Munro 1903-1994
Children
Phillip Alexander Judd 1928-2014
Louis Arthur Judd 1900-1973
Married 1924
Olive Grace May Judd 1903-1972
Married 1933
Eva Harrison 1920-1979
Charles Raymond Judd 1903-1959

Married	1937
Thelma Doris Tuit	1917-1991
Children	
Elsie Margaret Judd	1937-1990
Thelma Elizabeth Judd	1940-1984
Shirley Vivian Judd	1948-2019
Stephen Patrick Judd	1950-1990
Gregory Judd	1951-2022
Brian David Anthony Judd	1953-1969
James Walter Judd	1955-2001
Andrew John Judd	1957-2000
Horace James Richard Judd	1906-1983
married	1935
Hazel Myrtle Drakeford	1905-1974
children	
Lois Emma Judd	1936-2015
Married	1912
Edward Scott	1870-1937
Children	
Edward George Scott	1912-1981
Married	1933
Rose Marie Belleville	1912-1940
Children	
Graeme Edward Douglas Scott	1935-1988
Joyce Beverly Scott	1939-2007
Married	1952
Sylvia May Dempsey	1925-1978
Norman Douglas Scott	1917-1985
Married	1946
Phyllis Oldaker	1922-2014
John George Cornwill	1877–1956
Married	1900
Alice Lobb	1880-1967
Children	
William Joseph George Cornwill	1903–1989
Married	1927
Florence Lillian Eva Bartlett	1905-1990

Children	
Joyce Cornwill	
Raymond Cornwill	1905–1994
Married	1928
Jesse May Firth	1907-1996
Children	
Patricia Rosie Cornwill	1929-2016
Neville George James Cornwill	1931-2016
Edward Benjamin Cornwill	1906–1983
Ivy May Cornwill	1909–1996
Mary Ann Cornwill	1880–1963
Married	1900
George John Polson	1871-1946
Children	
Irene Myrtle Polson	1901-1979
Married	1918
Harry Wilfred Stevens	1858-1975
Children	
Henrietta Winifred Stevens	1918-1927
Henry Wilfred Stevens	1918-1929
Irene May Stevens	1919-1963
George Edward Polson	1902-1998
Married	1924
Jesse Ellen Ould	1906-1956
children	
James Henry Polson	1927-1966
James Burton Polson	1903-1937
Mavis Jean Polson	1917-2006
Married	1940
Thomas Joseph Spicer	1914-1973
Lucy Laura Cornwill	1882–1976
Married	1902
Alfred Daniel Harris	1874-1945
Children	
Alfred Leonard Harris	1903–1955

Married	1922
Eileen Amelia Roach	1905-1957
children	
Ronald Leslie Harris	?
Reginald Leonard Harris	1923-1923
Veronica June Harris	1924-2012
Dulcie May Harris	1909–1983
Married	1930
William Edward Roache	1898-1956
Children	
Rosie Wilma Roache	1930-2003
William Leonard Roache	1932-1985
Pamela Joy Roache	1942-2002
Bernard Leslie Harris	1913–1975
Edith Cornwill	1883–1883
Edward Richard Cornwill	1883–1883
Walter Cornwill	1885–1885
Ethel May Cornwill	1886–1969
Married	1905
Sydney Charles Carter	1883-1953
Children	
Charles Edward Carter	1905-1969
Ethel Carter	1910-1976
Ivy May Carter	1910-1996
Married	1940
Francis Allen Taylor	1909-1984
Jack Carter	1912-1986
Married	1933
Eva Maud Dunstan	1911-1961
Children	
Jean Margaret Carter	1933-1982
James Carter	1913-1995
Married	1938
Dorothy Maud Leggo	1910-1985
Margaret Carter	1915-2007
Married	
James Henry Cornish	1911-1993

Children	
Beverley Cornish	1940-2010
Walter Sydney Carter	1923-1941
Albert Richard Cornwill	1886–1954
Married	1917
Ruby Victoria Harris	1893-1952
Children	
William James Cornwill	1918-1918
William Leslie Richard Cornwill	1919-1921
Jessie Lucas Cornwill	1889–1890
Florence Ruby Cornwill	1891–1964
Married	1911
Frederick Gibbs	1883-1934
Children	
Ethel Gibbs	1912–1997
Married	1937
Edmond George Hector Warren	1903–1988
Children	
John Frederick Warren	1939-2023
Pearl May Gibbs	1914–1983
Married	1931
Murray Sydney Bush	1907-1983
Dorothy Gibbs	1915–
Frederick Charles Gibbs	1919–1979
Married	1944
Marjorie Noreen Jones	?-2009
Married	1945
William Charles Janetzki	1899-1978

George Perry

George Perry, who was the twin of Margaret Agnes Perry was born in Richmond Victoria on 28th June, 1851. When he was about a year old, the family moved to the Maryborough, Victoria area.

On 10th May 1873 George married Matilda Edwards at Presbyterian Church in Ballarat.

George was 21 and Matilda was just 16! They settled somewhere around Majorca, Victoria.

They had 5 children before they separated around 10 May 1888.

Sarah Jane Perry	1874–1935
Maud Perry	1877–1966
Ethel Perry	1880–1965
Frederick Charles Perry	1884–1929
William Ernest Perry	1887–1940

There was a notice in the Police Gazette as there was a warrant out for George's arrest. It's a great piece of history because it gives a good description of George.

GEORGE PERRY is charged, on warrant, with deserting his wife, Matilda Perry, at Majorca, in May, 1888. Description :—Miner, 37 years of age, 5 feet 8 inches high, fair complexion and hair, stout build, about 13 stone weight, two upper front teeth missing, a slight scar of long standing over right eye, caused by a fall of a quartz reef while mining. Supposed to be in Queensland.— O.7284. 19th August, 1889.

In 1889 Matilda filed for a divorce in the Supreme Court of Victoria. In her testimony she states that she is a Boarding House Keeper in Majorca, Victoria. She gives evidence that she hasn't seen George since their separation. Her testimony claims that George had an incestuous relationship with their daughter, Sarah Jane, when Sarah was just 13. There was a child born of the relationship (Albert). The petition does not state that the marriage was dissolved. Nor is there any further information about whether there was further legal proceedings against George.

George started to go by the alias Frederick Crew. The family moved to Charters Towers in Queensland. In 1890, Sarah's baby, Albert died there. George and Matilda had 2 more children in Queensland.

Eva May Perry   1891–1938
Alfred Percival James Perry   1894–1976

Here is a picture of Matilda and George.

There was a notice in the The Northern Miner in May 1923.

GOLDEN WEDDING.

CREW.—Mr. and Mrs. F. C. Crew, Bowen (late of Charters Towers), married at Ballarat. Falmouth, England, May 10th, 1873. Mother and father of Mrs. Kenna, Perth, West Australia; Mrs. J. Dunn, Melbourne; Mrs. A. H. Mederaf, Winton; Mrs. J. Troy, Charters Towers; Mr. Frederick Crew, Mr. William Crew and Mr. Alfred Crew, of Bowen.

George worked as a miner. They moved to Bowen and then to Brisbane where he died 22 July, 1926 and was buried at the Toowong Cemetery . Here is his obituary.

The death of Frederick Charles Crew, in Brisbane, on Thursday last, removed from our midst a resident of long standing. Deceased had spent most of his early years in Charters Towers, and reaped prosperity with so many others in the days when fortunes were dragged from the earth on that field. It was there that he reared a large family, who were a credit to him. Later on he came to Bowen and made a home. He also secured employment with the Town Council, and occupied the position of garbage remover until two years back when ill health compelled him to resign. Since then his health has continued to fail. It was under the belief that a change of climate would be beneficial that he decided to stay in Brisbane for a time. The late Mr Crew was about 80 years of age, and was one of those fine old pioneers who did so much in their day to blaze the tracks in the northern part of this State.

Matilda went to live with her daughter Maud and she died 4th December, 1941. Her obituary is to the right and a picture of her grave is below.

MRS. MATILDA CREW

The death occurred at the residence of her son-in-law in Elderslie Street on Thursday last of Mrs. Matilda Crew, aged 85 years.

Deceased was a native of the Old Country, born at Falmouth, County Cornwall in the south of England.

As Miss Matilda Edwards, after emigrating to Australia, she married Mr. F. C. Crew in Victoria, and they then came to Charters Towers, making their home there during the period of the '91 strike.

Mrs. Crew visited Winton in 1913 for a short period thence going to Bowen, Rockhampton and then to Brisbane. Her husband predeceased her in Brisbane in 1926.

For the last three years Mrs. Crew has been residing with her daughter and son-in-law, Mr. and Mrs. A. H. Medcraf, Winton.

She is survived by two daughters and one son, Mrs. A. H. Medcraf (Winton). Mrs. J. Dunne (Melbourne) and Mr. A. P. J. Crew (Clermont).

The last rites were performed by the Rev. R. Peel, the funeral leaving the Methodist Church at 4 p.m. on Friday.

George (Frederick) Perry (Crew)	1851-1926
Married	1873
Matilda Edwards	1856–1941
children	
Sarah Jane Perry (Crew)	1874–1935
Children	
Albert Perry (Crew)	1888–1890
Married	1900
Michael Kenna	1867–1945
Children	
John "Clarrie" Kenna	1918–1919
Maud Perry (Crew)	1877–1966
Married	1895
Arthur Henry Medcraf	1868–1943
Children	
Florence Matilda Medcraf	1896–1976
Married	1914
Wilfred West Parker	1890-1950
Children	
Wilfred Arthur Parker	1914-1919
Maud Barbara Parker	1919-2015
Henry West Parker	1922-2003
Doris Hilda May Medcraf	1898–1930
Married	1924
James Barrington Gregory	1896-1967
Ethel Perry	1880–1965
Married	1899
John Dunn	1875-1967
Children	
Ethel Matilda Dunn	1901-1925
Daisy Sarah May Dunn	1907-1977
Frederick Charles Augustus Perry (Crew) 1884–1929	
Married	1919
Myrtle Benstead	1898-1962
Children	
Edna Cecelia Dunn	1919-1974
Married	
Arthur Snow	1904-1969
Children	
Linda Jean Snow	1951-2017

William Ernest Perry (Crew)	1887–1940
Married	1908
Florence Francis Teague	1888-1985
Children	
Phyllis Francis Crew	1910-
Married	1927
Grahame Maltby Shardlow	1906-1998
Children	
Glen Grahame Shardlow	1943-1990
Ernest William Crew	1912-1963
Married	
Thelma Ellen Sorohan	1921-2008
Children	
May Francs Crew	1943-1995
Frederick Charles Crew	1944-1944
Eva May Perry	1891–1938
Married	1916
John Troy	1878-1959
Children	
Edna May Theresa Troy	1917-1990
Alfred Percival James Perry	1894–1976
Married	1920
Marjorie Ford	1904-1984
Children	
Marjorie Crew	1921-2000
Married	
Victor Stanley Gricks	1909-1981
Children	
Barbara Joyce Gricks	1945-1956
Stanley Gricks	1945
Elsie Maud Crew	1923-2004
Married	
George Clement Weatherhead	1916-1992
Children	
Neil Ronald Weatherhead	1951-2000
Frederick John James Crew	1925-1995
Dorothy Crew	1927-
Alfred Percival James Crew	1932-1976
Robert Crew	1935-1999
Noel Crew	1939-
Ronald Allan Crew	1942-2020

William Perry

William Perry was born in 1857 in Maryborough, Victoria.

On 24th August 1880, William married Jane Elizabeth Harris, in the Christ Church, Maryborough , the same church as Margaret and Edward . William was 23 and Jane was 21.

They had 13 children

William Robert Perry	1881–1902
Alfred Perry	1882–1942
Mabel Matilda Margaret Perry	1884–1914
Edward Richard Perry	1885–1887
Albert Charles Perry	1887–1913
Edmund Perry	1888–1953
John Francis Perry	1891–1959
Lucas Leslie Perry	1893–1963
Elizabeth Ellen Emma Perry	1895–1952
Olive Lavinia Perry	1897–1975
Clive S Perry	1897–
Thomas Percival Lyle Perry	1899–1988
Harte Gerald Perry	1901–1976

William and Jane lived in a 4 roomed weatherboard house on Commercial Road Majorca . William worked as a miner and a labourer. William died on 9 November 1918 and was buried in the Majorca Cemetery .

An old resident of Majorca, in the person of William Perry, passed away on Saturday last at the age of 62 years. Friends are notified that the funeral will leave his late residence for the Majorca cemetery this afternoon at 3 o'clock.

The following is the tree that William Perry created.

Alfred Perry	1882–1942
Married	1908
Elsie May Bell	1890-1945
Children:	
Percival George Perry	1908-1978
Mavis Annie Perry	1911-1976
Married	1929
Gordon Howard	1906-1982
Alfred and Elsie Divorced	1929
Alfred had 3 other children with Emma Jardine (1891-1951)	
Olive Joyce Perry	1917-?
Edwin Thomas Perry	1920-1980
Enlisted in WW2 military.	
Married	1942
Margaret Eileen Quarrell	1918-1958
Alfred George Perry	1821-?
Enlisted in WW2 military.	
Mabel Matilda Margaret Perry	1884–1914
Married	1908
Michael Hare	1874-1917
Children	
Wilfred Michael Thomas Hare	1908-?
Cecil Lucas Hare	1910-1970
Married	1945.
Bertha Josephine Mathews	1918-1989
Norman Jason Hare	1912-1913
Rosina Jane Elizabeth Hare	1913-1975
Lucy Hare	1914-1914
Edward Richard Perry	1885–1887
Albert Charles Perry	1887–1913
Edmund Augustus Perry	1889–1953
Married	1911
Ada Maud Mason	1888-1950
Children:	
Herbert William Perry	1912-1934

Ernest Malcolm Perry	1918-1983
Edmund George Perry	1934-1941
Allan John Perry	1939-1984
John Francis Perry	1891–1959
Married	1924
Mary Jane Dodson	1885-1963
Children	
William Robert Perry	1925-2008
Violet May Perry	1927-1978
Married	1948
Clarence William Cruse	1922-1973
Children:	
Judith Ann Cruse	1956-1987
Lucas Leslie Perry	1893–1963
Married	1917
Myrtle Ivy Cuy	1895-1971
Children	
Victory Trevena Perry	1918-2011
Married	1941
Michigan James Williams	1919-1997
Kenneth Maxwell Thomas Perry	1930-1976
Married Margery Elaine Drew	1931-2004
Vivian Doris Perry	1922-2015
Married Arthur William Howarth	1922-1977
William George Perry	?-1994
Elizabeth Ellen Emma Perry	1895–1952
Married	1924
McRobert Mathews	1902-1948
Children	
Charles Henry Mathews	1921-1967
Olive Lavinia Perry	1897–1975
Married	1930
Leslie John Tysoe	1930-1965
Children	
Leslie Thomas Tysoe	1930-2005
Henry William Tysoe	1939-2015
Charles Richard Tysoe	?
Clive S Perry	1897–

Thomas Percival Lyle Perry	1899–1988
Married	1926
Florence Victoria Fishlock	1901-1986
Children	
Florence May Perry	1932-1999
Harte Gerald Perry	1901–1976
Married	1923
Amy Ethel Warren	1906-1995
Children	
Harte Perry	1926-1996
Kevin George Perry	1928-1972

Boy Drowned in Baths

MARYBOROUGH, Sunday. — The fully-clothed body of Edmund George Perry, aged 7 years, was recovered from 10 feet of water in Maryborough baths yesterday afternoon, shortly after the close of the ceremonies in connection with the official opening of the baths. Efforts at resuscitation proved unsuccessful.

A puzzling feature is that despite the presence of many swimmers and a large crowd of spectators, no person saw the boy fall into the water. Four years ago the boy's elder brother was killed in an accidental fall of earth.

How can someone drown at the Baths when there are so many people around?

I would hazard a guess that because there was so many people in the water, all having a good time, that they just failed to notice a young boy in difficulties.

What a very sad affair.

John Perry

John Perry appears on many family trees, however, finding factual sources has been difficult. There is a few family trees that have John marrying and settling around the Woolongong area. I'm not convinced that is right, however, I could be wrong.

Most agree that John was born in 1862.

I found the following news article, which may belong to our John. I thought I would share it just in case.

It's a very sad story.

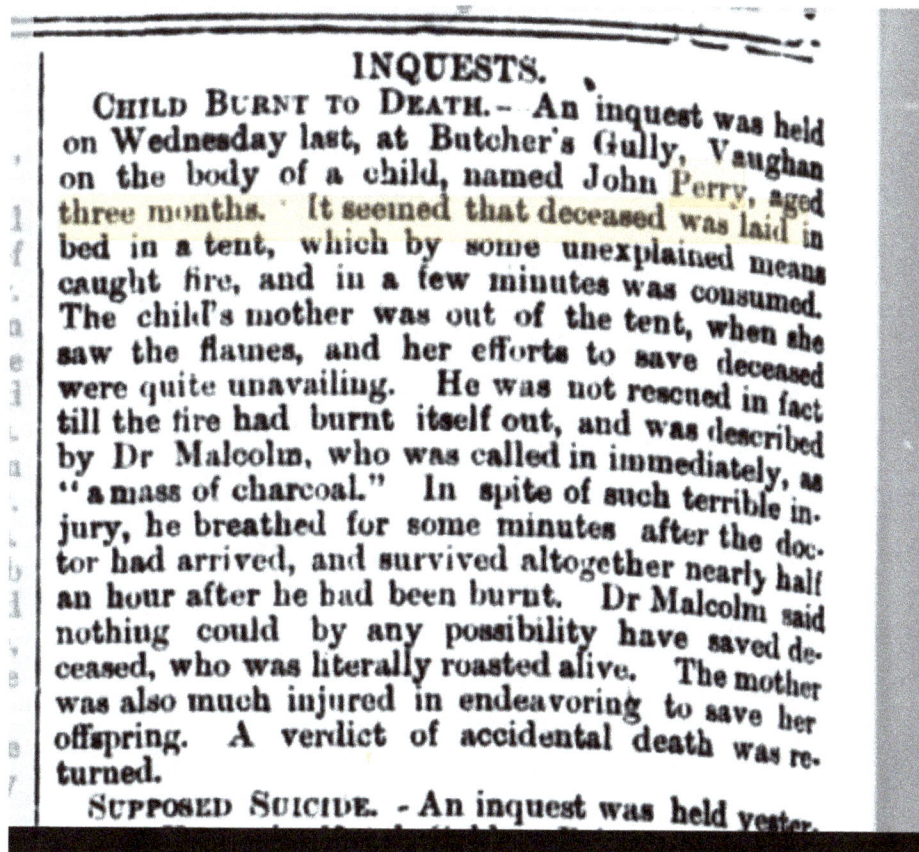

INQUESTS.

CHILD BURNT TO DEATH.- An inquest was held on Wednesday last, at Butcher's Gully, Vaughan on the body of a child, named John Perry, aged three months. It seemed that deceased was laid in bed in a tent, which by some unexplained means caught fire, and in a few minutes was consumed. The child's mother was out of the tent, when she saw the flames, and her efforts to save deceased were quite unavailing. He was not rescued in fact till the fire had burnt itself out, and was described by Dr Malcolm, who was called in immediately, as "a mass of charcoal." In spite of such terrible injury, he breathed for some minutes after the doctor had arrived, and survived altogether nearly half an hour after he had been burnt. Dr Malcolm said nothing could by any possibility have saved deceased, who was literally roasted alive. The mother was also much injured in endeavoring to save her offspring. A verdict of accidental death was returned.

SUPPOSED SUICIDE. - An inquest was held yester

Elizabeth Margaret Perry

Elizabeth Margaret (Edmund and Ellen's 9th child) was born in 1865 She married Joseph Soutter on 16th September, 1884 in Craigie, Victoria. They had 16 children

Maud Ellen Soutter	1885–1885
Joseph Edmund Soutter	1885–1885
William John Soutter	1886–1967
Edmund Walter Soutter	1887–1965
Eva Lillian Soutter	1889–1964
Walter Charles Soutter	1891–1892
Lydia May Soutter	1891–1923
Florence Lavinia Soutter	1892–1958
Edith Alice Soutter	1894–1988
Irene Myrtle Soutter	1895–1977
Maud Ella Soutter	1896–1897
Charles Frederick Soutter	1897–1952
Jessica Elizabeth Soutter	1899–1984
Edith Margaret Soutter	1901–1902
Vera Gladys Soutter	1903–1936
Harold Leonard Soutter	1904–1905

I found this interesting memoir of Lois Cairns (nee Soutter)

> My father, William John Soutter was the eldest of sixteen children born, ten survived, born to Joseph Walter Soutter and Elizabeth Perry. Most of the six who did not survive, including twins, were born with lung complaints.
>
> Elizabeth was an Irish Catholic and William a dour Scot and staunch Presbyterian, who was also a lay preacher in the church and the possessor of a fine bass voice. Elizabeth gave up her religion when she married William, but when she

In the Age on 28th January, 1898 the following article was found, mentioning Joseph Soutter.

district branch of the A.M.A. was held at Carisbrook, the president, Mr. W. H. Bishop, occupying the chair. The regulations of the Victorian Chamber of Mines were received, but not agreed with, exception being taken to the proposed conditions under which certificates of competency should issue to miners. · Mr. D. Tuxworth was elected president, Mr. Joseph Soutter vice-president, and Mr. Charles Sainsbury re-elected secretary.

Joseph worked as a miner and later he was employed by the Railway. The family lived in Argyle Street, Maryborough and later lived in Fraser Street. In 1934, Elizabeth was living at 9 Carrick Street, Maryborough.

Joseph died 23rd April, 1926 and was buried in the Maryborough Cemetery. On 21st May, 1937 Margaret died and she was buried in the Maryborough Cemetery.

Elizabeth Margaret Perry (1865-1937) married **Joseph Walter Soutter** (1862-1926) in 1884

Children

Maud Ellen Soutter	1885–1885
Joseph Edmund Soutter	1885–1885
William John Soutter	1886–1967
Married	1912
Mary 'Polly' Elma Comber	1888-1972

    Children

Eunice Myrtle Soutter	1913-2001
Married	1937
George William Griffin Reeve	906-1982
Elma Jean Soutter	1917-1991
Married	1947
Louis Dressing	1917-2008
Margaret Lois Heather Soutter	1927-2009
Married	1948
Ronald Albert Cairns	**1925-1922**

Edmund Walter Soutter (1887–1965) married **Rose Hannah Brown** (1883-1909) in 1907.

Children

Harold Leslie Soutter	1908-1973
Married	1928
Doris Letitia Cooke	1908-1983

There were children, however, I don't have their details recorded.

Minnie Amelia Jamieson	1912-1972
Partner (no marriage found)	

    children

Robert Leslie Soutter	1940-2018
Valda Lorraine Soutter	1942-1948
Kaye Lynette Soutter	1943-2003
Donald Lindsay Soutter	1945-1976
Jenny Louise Soutter	1947-2016

Joseph Walter Soutter (unsure of his mother) 1912-1951

Married	1938
Edith Olive Daly	1914-1997

    Children

Raymond Fitzgerald Soutter	1939-1985
Elsie Soutter	1943-

Married	1918
Bertha Elizabeth Hornsby	1887-1984
Children	
Lindsay Edmund Soutter	1918-1960
Colin Douglas Soutter	1921-1973
Keith Alexander Soutter	1922-2005
Eric Victor Soutter	1924-2001
Lorna Lydia Soutter	1926-2017
Eva Lillian Soutter	1889–1964
Married	1908
Edmund Oppy	1888-1969
Children	
Thomas James Joseph Oppy	1909-1979
Charles Edmund Oppy	1913-1989
Harold William Oppy	1920-1021
Walter Charles Soutter	1891–1892
Lydia May Soutter	1891–1923
Married	1909
Percival James Stewart Quick	1889-1923
Children	
Harold Joseph Nathaniel Quick	1909–1971
Percival Charles James Quick	1910–1986
William Frederick Joseph Quick	1912–1988
Dulcie Lydia May Quick	1914–
James Stewart Quick	1915–1996
Robert Allan Quick	1918–1957
Isabell Joyce Quick	1921–1981
Florence Lavinia Soutter	1892–1958
Married	1917
Greig Quick	1896-1964
Children	
Mavis Eunice Quick	1914-1972
Raymond Ernest Quick	1918-2013
Florence Elizabeth Quick	1919-1984
Marie Jean Quick	1927-2004

Edith Alice Soutter	1894–1988
Married	1917
John Thomas Farley	1892-1972
Irene Myrtle Soutter	1895–1977
Married	1913
William John Sinclair	1890-1965
Children	
Ronald Charles Sinclair	1915-1986
Phyllis Doreen Sinclair	1917-1998
Leslie William Leigh	1920-1985
Maud Ella Soutter	1896–1897
Charles Frederick Soutter	1897–1952
married	1917
Alma Monica Bradley	1898-?
Children	
Joseph Samuel Soutter	1917-1983
John Charles Soutter	1919-2003
Francis Harry Soutter	1921-1997
Jessica Elizabeth Soutter	1899–1984
married	1922
William John Thompson	1871-1981
Edith Margaret Soutter	1901–1902
Vera Gladys Soutter	1903–1936
married	1925
Leslie White	?
Harold Leonard Soutter	1904–1905

Ellen Perry

Ellen, Edmund and Ellen's 10th child was born 10th August, 1866 in Maryborough, Victoria. At the age of 23, In august, 1889, she married Charles August Fawcett in Maryborough. Charles was born in Linton, Victoria around 1867.

They lived in Majorca, where he worked as a miner until around 1818 when they moved to Ballarat and he found work on the railway. Royce served in the first world war and was wounded in France.

Charles died 4th June, 1935 and Ellen died in 1953. They are buried in Ballarat.

Ellen and Charles created the following tree.

Ellen Perry	1866-1953
married	1889
Charles August Fawcett	1867-1935
Children	
Edmund Fawcett	1890–1890
Alice Fawcett	1891–1892
Charles Augustus II Fawcett	1893–1895
James Joseph I Fawcett	1896–1965
married	1915
May Eileen Ellis	1898-1952
children	
James Joseph Fawcett	1916-1919
Eileen May Fawcett	1918-1998
Kathleen Ellen Fawcett	1920-2002
Vera Lillian Fawcett	1923-2007
Walter Charles Patrick Fawcett	1925-2000
Ellen Gladys Fawcett	1896–1959
married	1917
Charles Henry Strathmore Shuttleworth	1891-1960
children	
Henry Charles Shuttleworth	1917-
Royce Fawcett	1899–1969
married	1925
Lydia Olive Gloster	1903-1974
children	
Eunice Jean Fawcett	1927-2012
Matilda Muriel Fawcett	1901–1996
married	1923
Charles Henry Jones	1895-1974

Children	
Ruth Jones	1934-2018
Baden Jones	1938-2015
Myra Florence Fawcett	1906–
Married	1930
Walter Alfred Crompton	1907-1969
Children	
Ivan Walter Crompton	1938-1992
Eric Charles Fawcett	1909–1942
married	1940
Gladys May Archibald	

Charles Perry

Charles Perry, Ellen and Edmund's 11th child was born 7th March, 1869. He married Susanah Kezia Judd , another local girl from Maryborough, in 1893. They had one child, a daughter, Charlotte Rose who didn't live past 1 year of age.

Charles was a Brickmaker and the couple lived in Talbot Road, Maryborough for many years.

Charles died 18 September, 1949 and Susanah died 1st September, 1960. They are buried in the Maryborough Cemetery.

Charles Perry	1869-1949
Married	1893
Susanah Kezia Judd	1872-1960
Children	
Charlotte Rose	?

Sarah Ann Perry

Sarah Ann Perry, Edmund and Ellen's youngest child was born in 1874. When she was 16 years old, she married John Robert Judd in Maryborough in 1890. John was the older brother of Susanah Kezia Judd, who married Sarah's brother Charles.

John died in 1892 and was buried in Maryborough.

In 1893, Sarah married Francis Hugh Randall. Francis was born in Amherst 1875. A year later, in 1894, twins were born: Mary Kathleen and Lilly.

In 1895 Sarah was imprisoned for 2 months for being Idle and disorderly. The prison records describe her as being 5feet 1inch, Fresh complexion, brown hair and blue eyes. She had a small scar on the palm of her right hand. She had no previous convictions.

There was a small piece in the Ballarat Star on 5th July 1895 about Sarah.

of the proceedings in Parliament.

As mentioned in yesterday's *Star*, the Ballarat East Police in their desire to rid the town of objectionable characters arrested three women named Sarah Morton, Catherine Wall, and Sarah Randall. The accused were brought before Mr Leader, P.M., and Messrs Williams, Elsworth, Miller, Phillips, Josephs, and Larter, J's.P., at the Town Police Court yesterday charged with vagrancy. Inspector Hamilton at the outset stated that the woman Randall had only recently been discharged from the Ballarat Gaol, and as she intended to go to Maryborough he thought it only fair that she should be given another chance. The accused, who had a child in her arms, promised to leave Ballarat at once, and the magistrates discharged her with the understanding that Plain-clothes Constable M'Pherson should see her off by the train that day. The other women at their request were remanded for a week. Bail was fixed in two sureties of £50

In 1899, Sarah had another baby, Maud Ellen, who died the same year.

In 1990 Sarah died. There is child also documented as having born and died in 1990. Perhaps they died in childbirth.

Francis didn't remarry, but he moved to Carlton and worked as a baker. He enlisted in 1915 and was killed in action on 1st October, 1915 at Gallipoli. He is buried at Shrapnel Valley Cemetery and there his name is on the war memorial in Canberra.

Here is Sarah's contribution to the Perry tree.

Sarah Ann Perry	1874-1900
married	1890
John Robert Judd	1866-1892
Married	1893
Francis Hugh Randall	1875-1915
children	
Mary Kathleen Randall	1894-1936
married	1917
Frederick Parker	1887-1936
children	
Rhoda May Parker	1918-2006
Leslie Gordon Parker	1919-
Stanley Parker	?
Maud Ellen Randall	1898-1899
Sarah Ann Randall	1899-1899

Index of Names

Annear	Eveline	1878-1963
Baker	Myrtle Rose	1901-1978
Bartlett	Florence Lillian Eva	1905-1990
Belleville	Rose Marie	1912-1940
Benstead	Myrtle	1898-1962
Brogan	Henry	1886-1974
Brogan	Ellen (Doris) May	1910-1980
Brogan	Olga May	1917-1917
Brogan (Tunes)	Leslie (Peter)	1915-1978
Brown	George William	1874-1932
Brown	William Edward	1894-1965
Brown	Myrtle Rose	1921-2005
Brown	Edna	1922-2007
Brown	Harold	1900-1969
Brown	Dorothy Joan	1924-1983
Brown	Leonard George	1903-1978
Brown	Dorothy Lynette	1931-1988
Bush	Murray Sydney	1907-1983
Carter	Sydney Charles	1883-1953
Carter	Charles Edward	1905-1969
Carter	Ethel	1910-1976
Carter	Ivy May	1910-1996
Carter	Jack	1912-1986
Carter	Jean Margaret	1933-1982
Carter	James	1913-1995
Carter	Margaret	1915-2007
Carter	Walter Sydney	1923-1941
Cornish	James Henry	1911-1993
Cornish	Beverley	1940-2010
Cornwall	Edward	1904-1972
Cornwall	Benjamin James	1869–1943
Cornwell	Edward	1849-1914

Cornwell	Frederick Rupert	1902-1902
Cornwell	William charles	1871–1913
Cornwell	Edward Richard Francis	1872–1882
Cornwill	Doris Irene	1899-
Cornwill	Albert Richard	1891-1929
Cornwill	Albert Raymond	1918-1979
Cornwill	William Charles	1920-1998
Cornwill	Walter James	1922-1977
Cornwill	Violet Jean	1927-2016
Cornwill	James Leslie	1892-1985
Cornwill	James William	1917-1917
Cornwill	Irene Harriet	1922-1945
Cornwill	Jean Emma	1923-1924
Cornwill	Frederick Bert	1926-1989
Cornwill	Lillian Myrtle	1893-1935
Cornwill	Margaret	1895-1947
Cornwill	William Robert	1896-1916
Cornwill	John Raymond	1898-1978
Cornwill	Helen Veronica	1920-1993
Cornwill	Thelma Violet	1922-1981
Cornwill	Doris Margaret	1923-1969
Cornwill	John Walter	1926-1993
Cornwill	Walter Henry	1902-1974
Cornwill	Mavis	1930-2005
Cornwill	Graham	1939-1939
Cornwill	Margaret	1940-1999
Cornwill	Bertie	1905-1941
Cornwill	Constance	1939-
Cornwill	Leonard	1900–1900
Cornwill	Violet	1908–1912
Cornwill	Ellen Lucas	1874–1912
Cornwill	Alice Marion Hollis	1901-1997

Cornwill	Margaret Jane	1876–1959
Cornwill	John George	1877–1956
Cornwill	William Joseph George	1903–1989
Cornwill	Joyce	
Cornwill	Raymond	1905–1994
Cornwill	Patricia Rosie	1929-2016
Cornwill	Neville George James	1931-2016
Cornwill	Edward Benjamin	1906–1983
Cornwill	Ivy May	1909–1996
Cornwill	Mary Ann	1880–1963
Cornwill	Lucy Laura	1882–1976
Cornwill	Edith	1883–1883
Cornwill	Edward Richard	1883–1883
Cornwill	Walter	1885–1885
Cornwill	Ethel May	1886–1969
Cornwill	Albert Richard	1886–1954
Cornwill	William James	1918-1918
Cornwill	William Leslie Richard	1919-1921
Cornwill	Jessie Lucas	1889–1890
Cornwill	Florence Ruby	1891–1964
Cox	Florence Alexandra	1903-1994
Crew	Phyllis Francis	1910-
Crew	Ernest William	1912-1963
Crew	May Francis	1943-1995
Crew	Frederick Charles	1944-1944
Crew	Marjorie	1921-2000
Crew	Elsie Maud	1923-2004
Crew	Frederick John James	1925-1995
Crew	Dorothy	1927-
Crew	Alfred Percival James	1932-1976
Crew	Robert	1935-1999
Crew	Noel	1939-

Crew	Ronald Allan	1942-2020
Cuy	Jessie	1898-1974
Dempsey	Sylvia May	1925-1978
Drakeford	Hazel Myrtle	1905-1974
Dunn	John	1875-1967
Dunn	Ethel Matilda	1901-1925
Dunn	Daisy Sarah May	1907-1977
Dunn	Edna Cecelia	1919-1974
Dunstan	Eva Maud	1911-1961
Edwards	Matilda	1856–1941
Firth	Jesse May	1907-1996
Ford	Marjorie	1904-1984
Fraser	Samuel	1905-1984
Garlepp	Gloria Mena	1918-2015
Gibbs	Frederick	1883-1934
Gibbs	Ethel	1912–1997
Gibbs	Pearl May	1914–1983
Gibbs	Dorothy	1915–
Gibbs	Frederick Charles	1919–1979
Gibson	Blanche Lillian	1895-1942
Gormely	Ellen	1831-1905
Greenshaw	Thelma Olive	1905-1996
Gregory	James Barrington	1896-1967
Gricks	Victor Stanley	1909-1981
Gricks	Barbara Joyce	1945-1956
Gricks	Stanley	1945
Grossman	Harry Trevena	1899-1965
Harris	Emily	1867-1943
Harris	Alfred Daniel	1874-1945
Harris	Alfred Leonard	1903–1955
Harris	Ronald Leslie	
Harris	Reginald Leslie	1923-1923
Harris	Veronica June	1924-2012

Harris	Dulcie May	1909–1983		Mohr	Doris Ines	1930
Harris	Bernard Leslie	1913–1975		Munro	Ida Mary	1903-1994
Harris	Ruby Victoria	1893-1952		Oldaker	Phyllis	1922-2014
Harrison	Eva	1920-1979		Ould	Jesse Ellen	1906-1956
Howe	Ellen Veronica	1899-1960		Parker	Wildred West	1890-1950
Janetzki	William Charles	1899-1978		Parker	Wildred Arthur	1914-1919
Jones	Marjorie Noreen	?-2009		Parker	Maud Barbara	1919-2015
Judd	James Phillip	1886-1909		Parker	Henry West	1922-2003
Judd	John Phillip	1898-1961		Perry	Margaret Agnes	1851-1926
Judd	Phillip Alexander	1928-2014		Perry	Edmund	1825-1896
Judd	Louis Arthur	1900-1973		Perry	George	1801-1847
Judd	Olive Grace May	1903-1972		Perry	Edmund	1765-1801
Judd	Charles Raymond	1903-1959		Perry	Ann	1828-1905
Judd	Elsie Margaret	1937-1990		Perry	Sarah	1830-1904
Judd	Thelma Elizabeth	1940-1984		Perry	Mary	1832-
Judd	Shirley Vivian	1948-2019		Perry	George	1833-1889
Judd	Gregory	1951-2022		Perry	Martha	1834
Judd	Brian David Anthony	1953-1969		Perry	Maria	1835-1872
Judd	James Walter	1955-2001		Perry	Mary	1837-1918
Judd	Andrew John	1957-2000		Perry	Elizabeth	1840-1881
Judd	Horace James Richard	1906-1983		Perry	Martha	1842-
Judd	Lois Emma	1936-2015		Perry	George	
Judd	Stephen Patrick	1950-1990		Perry	Mary Jane	1855-1869
Kelly	Lorna Mabel	1922-2011		Perry	William	1857-1918
Kenna	Michael	1867–1945		Perry	Edward	1859-1860
Kenna	John "Clarrie"	1918–1919		Perry	James	1861-1861
Leggo	Dorothy Maud	1910-1985		Perry	Elizabeth Margaret	1865-1937
Lobb	Alice	1880-1967		Perry	Ellen	1866-1953
Medcraf	Arthur Henry	1868–1943		Perry	Charles	1869-1947
Medcraf	Doris Hilda May	1898–1930		Perry	Edmond	1871-1890
Medcraf	Florence Matilda	1896–1976				

Perry	Sarah Ann	1874-1900
Perry	Maud	1877–1966
Perry	Ethel	1880–1965
Perry	Frederick Charles Augustus	1884–1929
Perry	William Ernest	1887–1940
Perry	Eva May	1891–1938
Perry	Alfred Percival James	1894–1976
Polson	George John	1871-1946
Polson	Irene Myrtle	1901-1979
Polson	George Edward	1902-1998
Polson	James Henry	1927-1966
Polson	James Burton	1903-1937
Polson	Mavis Jean	1917-2006
Roach	Eileen Amelia	1905-1957
Roache	William Edward	1898-1956
Roache	Rosie Wilma	1930-2003
Roache	William Leonard	1932-1985
Roache	Pamela Joy	1942-2002
Scott	Edward	1870-1937
Scott	Edward George	1912-1981
Scott	Graeme Edward Douglas	1935-1988
Scott	Joyce Beverly	1939-2007
Scott	Norman Douglas	1917-1985
Shardlow	Grahame Maltby	1906-1998
Shardlow	Glen Grahame	1943-1990
Snow	Arthur	1904-1969
Snow	Linda Jean	1951-2017
Sorohan	Thelma Ellen	1921-2008
Spicer	Thomas Joseph	1914-1973
Stevens	Harry Wilfred	1858-1975
Stevens	Henrietta Winifred	1918-1927
Stevens	Henry Wilfred	1918-1929
Stevens	Irene may	1919-1963
Taylor	Francis Allen	1909-1984
Teague	Florence Francis	1888-1985
Troy	John	1878-1959
Troy	Edna May Theresa	1917-1990
Tuit	Thelma Doris	1917-1991
Tunes	Leslie John	1936-2016
Tunes	Lillian Myrtle	1937-
Tunes	Donald Lawrence	1939-
Tunes	Janice Marlene	1940-
Warren	Edmond George Hector	1903–1988
Warren	John Frederick	1939-2023
Weatherhead	George Clement	1916-1992
Weatherhead	Neil Ronald	1951-2000